YOUTH
EVANGELISM

YOUTH EVANGELISM

David R. Veerman

VICTOR BOOKS®

A DIVISION OF SCRIPTURE PRESS PUBLICATIONS INC.
USA CANADA ENGLAND

Scripture references, unless otherwise indicated, are from the *Holy Bible, New International Version*, ©1973, 1978, 1984, International Bible Society. Used by permission of Zondervan Bible Publishers.

Recommended Dewey Decimal Classification: 155.5
Suggested Subject Heading: ADOLESCENCE

Library of Congress Catalog Card Number: 88-60219
ISBN: 0-89693-569-8

CONTENTS

85416

*To Jack Hamilton, Bill Eakin, and Clayton Baumann—
creative and courageous youth ministry pioneers
and extraordinary evangelists.*

FOREWORD

What this world needs is more people with *heart trouble*—not the kind that sends you to the cardiologist, but the kind that sends you to your knees!

There is a growing army of adults who have spiritual heart trouble over lost young people. It's an unexplainable hurt you feel when you see teenagers cruising aimlessly through the mall . . . pouring out of a local school . . . wasting their lives on the street. This heart trouble can be triggered by a headline announcing another teenage suicide or a look into young eyes that say, "I just don't care anymore."

If you have that heart condition that pulls you toward lost kids, you have picked up the right book. It tells you in clear, practical terms what to *do* with what you *feel*. The emphasis is not on the "shoulds" of reaching teenagers; it is cover-to-cover "hows." This book is, in a sense, a call to arms.

There is a battle raging for a generation–the kids we passed today. The enemy seems to have focused his attack on young people with one objective in mind: *to spiritually neutralize one entire generation.* If the devil can create one generation without God, he can have all the generations that follow.

He is gaining ground rapidly. In 25 years of youth ministry, I have never known a time when lost kids *knew less about Jesus,* or when Christian kids *cared less about living for Him.*

But the enemy is not the only one with plans for today's teenagers. God seems to have called them to help spark His last great revival on this planet: " 'In the last days,' " God says, " 'I will pour out My Spirit on all people. Your *sons and daughters* will prophesy, your *young men* will see visions' " (Acts 2:17, italics added).

The battle lines are drawn. And we who care about reaching teenagers for Christ are the *frontline troops!* The enemy is fighting with formidable weapons of music, media, doomsday thinking, brightly packaged sin, and family erosion. We dare not show up on the battlefield with antiquated weapons and no battle plan.

God has entrusted us with the exhilarating challenge of crossing generations with the Gospel. How shall we respond? It will require a willingness to change where needed and a commitment to creativity. If we try to reach this exploding generation the same old way, we will be talking to the same old people.

In *Youth Evangelism*, Dave Veerman gives us a *tested battle plan*. He is no "armchair general," sitting in an office theorizing about youth evangelism. For over 25 years, the author has been a frontlines combat soldier. He is one of Youth for Christ's most respected, most creative leaders. What Dave Veerman presents is what he *lives*. You will find him today where he has always been—reaching lost teenagers where they are. He has an incurable case of "heart trouble."

You probably would never have picked up this book unless you too had that heart trouble. As you read, ask the Lord of the harvest to give you vehicles for that burden of your heart. He will. As you struggle over who will bring Christ to the hurting kids in your community, listen for His voice. He may be calling you.

The teenagers who *never* hear the Gospel, who *never* attend a Christian meeting—*they* must become our magnificent obsession. When we allow our broken heart to say, "Lord, *whatever it takes* to reach them," the flame is kindled.

When Christ wanted to reach us, He did not set up a meeting "at His place" and ask us to come. He came to our meeting . . . "the Word became flesh and dwelt among us" (John 1:14, KJV). We would never have to come to His world, He came to ours.

As His representatives to young people, we must minister in this same "I'll come where *you* are" spirit. Our preaching and our program must go to their world, focus on life as they live it, identify with their need.

They are a generation hungry for a Leader, a Liberator—a

Saviour. We need only to present Christ in their language, and multitudes will follow Him. To succeed in "Mission: Youth" is to capture the future for Christ. To fail is too costly to calculate.

There is a place for you in this battle for a generation. And you can make a difference. Amy Carmichael calls us to enlist with these challenging words, "We will have all eternity to celebrate our victories . . . but only a few short hours to win them."

We are living in those "few short hours."

Ron Hutchcraft, Director
Metropolitan Youth for Christ
New York

CHAPTER ONE

Childish Ways

Walk with me through the doors of an average high school. The halls are empty, but teachers' voices float through open classroom doors. Posters and banners pepper beige walls with reminders of upcoming activities—class elections, dance squad tryouts, band rehearsals, and the fall play.

Suddenly, like a shrill alarm, the passing bell rings in our ears. Students respond by pouring into the halls. Books and three-ring binders fill their arms as they move singly or in clusters . . . or in couples. The echoes of the bell and the first steps on tile are soon covered by a crescendo of laughing, talking, and shouting voices, and the sound of shuffling Reeboks and Keds. For many it is lunchtime, and they crowd their way in line toward the day's special.

Following the lunch crowd into the cafeteria, we are greeted by the greasy scent of pizza, hot dogs, and fries. Heads turn to us but quickly return to the more pressing concerns: boys, girls, music, dates, parties, tests . . . and food. A visual survey reveals groups clustered about the room. The "in-crowd" of senior ball players and cheerleaders take the tables near the door. Along one wall are punkers, in full costume. Near the opposite wall, a chess set is pulled out and placed among the brown bags. In between are sophomore girls, junior jocks, "Skoal brothers," and other assorted cliques. The public address background music is punctuated by an announcement or two . . . but no one is listening.

Suddenly a pad of butter flies upward, catapulted by unseen hands. Just as suddenly, however, the guilty party is apprehended by a teacher and marched unceremoniously to the office.

Anticipating the bell, students deposit their garbage and trays in the appropriate bins and move toward the exits. At the ringing signal, they move out as their replacements fill the room.

We also leave, having tasted a small slice of high school life . . . on the surface. Beneath the facade of scrubbed faces, designer clothes, lettermen, proms, cheers, and grades lurks real campus life—thoughts, emotions, dreams, fears, insecurities, and potentials.

CAUGHT IN THE MIDDLE

Adolescence means change and challenge. Transforming bodies and minds raise questions and push their owners to find answers. Suspended between child and adult, high schoolers are caught in the middle. They want to grow up, to be trusted and treated as mature individuals, and to make their own decisions. But they also want the benefits of being at home with food, a room, and an allowance. Moving toward independence, kids test the limits of parents and other adult "rule-setters." Arguments over studies, curfew, household responsibilities, driving privileges, and dates are common.

But little boys and girls do not become men and women overnight. The transition is filled with anxious wonderings, mysterious changes, roller-coaster feelings, and countless mirror inspections. This exhausting process engulfs the teenage years and often begets trauma and a whole new vocabulary

---

LOST GENERATIONS

In the 1950s, teenagers *lost their innocence*. Liberated from their parents by music, movies, cars, and money, they discovered the meaning of freedom—and the meaning of guilt as a result of that freedom.

In the '60s, they *lost their authority*. All answers were challenged, and parents, religion, and the government were called into question. Young people were left with nothing in which to believe.

In the '70s, they *lost their love*. This was the "me" decade, dominated by words, phrases, and book titles beginning with "self." Families broke, and kids hungry for love settled for sex. They learned practically everything about sex and forgot practically everything about love.

Today, in the 1980s, young people have *lost hope*. Stripped of their innocence, authority, and love, teenagers stopped believing in the future, living as though there would not be one. Suicide has become the second greatest cause of death among young people.

Summary of an analysis by Ron Hutchcraft
(Youth For Christ Director for Metro New York).

---

for parents . . . peer pressure, cliques, rebellion, and "everybody's doing it."

While squeezed from without by parents and peers, adolescents are also pressured from within as they struggle to answer questions about themselves . . . "Who am I? Where do I fit in? What's good about me?" But even these questions are merely symptoms; the struggle for personal identity is deep, strong, and pervasive.

"When I was a child, I talked like a child, I thought like a child, I reasoned like a child. When I became a man, I put childish ways behind me" (1 Corinthians 13:11).

What is a child? And when does a person become an adult?

> Today's youth is a special kind. This kind has never known a newspaper without a war headline. This kind has had the opportunity to see right on television open pornography and smut unknown to any age. This kind has seen sin unbridled and marching across our nation with "respectability." This kind has experienced the alternative lifestyle suggestion—Adam and Eve and Steve. This kind knows all about cocaine and marijuana and all about the drug culture. This kind knows all about disobedience and getting off with it.
>
> Dr. E.V. Hill, in *Discipling the Young Person*, Paul Fleischmann, editor (San Bernardino, Calif.: Here's Life Publishers, Inc., 1985).

A few generations ago, the line was clear. Boys and girls grew up, got married, left home, and entered the "real world." With a growing emphasis on higher education, careers, and "finding oneself," this maturity border became difficult to define. Then there was the burgeoning crop of post-war babies. Soon sociologists began to talk about "teenagers" as an identifiable group within society.

In many ways, American culture began to revolve around teens, focusing advertising campaigns, entertainment, and fashions around their needs and tastes. And the high school became the funnel of the community, the common experience of nearly everyone. Scan the pages of any neighborhood newspaper and you will see that the high school is a strong focus of community interest.

With this growing population and increased attention (and ready access to money and cars) came the loss of innocence. Experiencing adult-sized pressures, children grew up faster than their parents, and high schoolers began to struggle with sex, alcohol, drugs, and stress.

Today these problems have been pushed down the age ladder even further. It is not uncommon to read of junior highers (12–14 years of age) and younger children involved in drugs, truancy, and crime. In this age of information, with television and movie shows, radio disc jockeys, and rock musicians preaching a hedonistic brand of morality, childhood is lost. Kids are too old, too soon.

An unexpected knock at the front door brought me face-to-face with Brad. He told me he had to talk to someone. Over the next hour or two, Brad slowly poured out his feelings of depression and loneliness. He felt rejected by girls and avoided by the in-crowd—a complete social misfit. Confused and unsure of himself, this maturing sophomore didn't know who he was or where he fit. Was he a Romeo? He wanted desperately to date. Was he an athlete? Going out for basketball was a live option, and "jocks" were "in" at East High. Was he a good student? The report card wasn't too promising. Was he a socialite? Basically shy, a few beers would bolster his confidence at parties. Brad was struggling and suffering. And he's not alone.

● Dan wonders if he'll keep playing football. He started on the sophomore team, but this year some of his friends have grown and have improved their skills. He figures to ride the bench and questions whether it's worth it.

● Most of her friends have been dating for at least a year—not so with Trisha. A tall girl with a "difficult" complexion, she wonders if she'll ever go out.

● Music is very important to Mike, especially hard rock. He

"Who am I?" the young adolescent asks again and again. In this search for identity, an adolescent depends heavily on the reactions and perceptions of others. Why? Adolescents tend to see themselves as others see them. When affirmed as significant individuals, adolescents see themselves as people who are respected; they begin to feel good about themselves.

Five Cries of Parents, Merton P. and A. Irene Strommen (San Francisco: Harper & Row, 1985).

tends to be a loner and just hangs out with a few friends who are into the same bands. His parents and teachers don't seem to care much, and so he drifts further away from school.

• Sally's parents are college-graduated professionals, and they have high hopes for their eldest. Grades are very important. Geometry, however, mystifies Sally, and she dreads Dad's reaction to her latest test score.

These young people want desperately to be accepted by friends and important others in the pecking order. This desire to belong, to be part of the party, brings to young people a myriad of moral dilemmas, often in direct conflict with their parents' and churches' expectations. "Come on, try it!" and "Everyone's doing it!" and other not-so-subtle lines urge involvement with alcohol, drugs, sex, and other assorted taboos.

• Cheri went to her first important party as a sophomore. She felt honored to be with the older, popular kids. That's when she had her first drink. At first she felt guilty, but then, at subsequent parties, it got to be a habit. She liked the way it made her feel, and she liked being part of the group.

• The locker room talk added to the pressure Tom felt as he slipped his arm around Jennifer. He knew the guys would ask "what he got" that night. And she really turned him on. His mind raced, searching for convincing words to tell her.

I've met hundreds of Brads, Dans, Trishas, Mikes, Sallys, Cheris, and Toms. I remember their struggles. They're normal kids moving through adolescence. But there are other kids, with special needs, who also imprint my memory.

The Loner

Sunday morning my college dining hall buzzed with the word that Sam was dead, found hanging in his dorm room. Sam and I had played intramural basketball together, but I didn't *really* know him. He was a loner, keeping his thoughts (and his despair) to himself.

The Silent

One peaceful summer afternoon, calm, clean suburbia was rocked by the news that a high school junior had systematically murdered his entire family. When questioned, school counselors replied that Roger was a quiet student who had never caused any problems. In fact, his grades were good, and he was active in band.

The Shy
An honor-roll student from a strong Christian home, Susan was well liked by those who knew her. Nice looking and pleasant, she seemed normal, but she fell apart emotionally during her first month at college. Years later, Susan continues to be hospitalized for emotional problems.

The Desperate
Only a few of her closest friends knew the real reason for René's absence. Everyone else assumed she was sick or on vacation. Not even her boyfriend, the potential father-to-be, knew she was pregnant. René had an abortion. Now she lives with the mental and emotional scars.

A GENERATION IN TROUBLE
Sam, Roger, Susan, and René had much in common. They were quiet young people whose calm exteriors hid churning emotions which eventually erupted, destroying lives. But there was also another common denominator—all four were within reach of help from Christian friends, adults, and minis-

---

SUICIDE

In the last 35 years, there has been an increase of almost 800 percent among teenagers under age 15 committing suicide. Approximately 300 youngsters killed themselves last year. In 1950, there were fewer than 40.

From a recent report published by Metropolitan Life Insurance Company.

ters. But they were invisible—unseen and unreached.
Consider these facts:
• Suicide is the second leading cause of death of high-school-age young people, claiming thousands every year.
• Alcohol, cocaine, and "crack"—substance abuse in general—is epidemic as kids drug themselves for pleasure or escape.
• "Sex abuse" produces a harvest of young mothers and a holocaust of abortions.
• The drop-out rate steadily rises.
• "Runaways," "throwaways," "abused children," and "latchkey kids" are clichés, well-worn descriptions of grim realities.

The truth is that young people are in trouble. This is a generation at risk . . . pressured, lost, confused, searching, and hurting. And they are going to hell!

Beneath the startling headlines or graphic statistics are real

---

YOUTH CULTURE STATISTICS

Runaways: One million youth in 1986 ran away from home. (Official estimate of the Administration of Children, Youth, and Families, HHS)

Leading Causes of Death: 1) Accidents (19,161); 2) Suicide (5,121); Homicide (4,772) (Figures for ages 15 to 24 years, National Health Statistics Center, 1985)

Drug and Alcohol Problems: Over three million 12- to 17-year-olds were drug users in 1985. (National Institute on Drug Abuse) Some 4.6 million 14- to 17-year-olds used alcohol regularly in 1986. (National Clearinghouse for Alcohol Information)

Source: A *Teen Vision* report, December 1987

About one million teenagers become pregnant each year with about four out of ten ending in abortion.

Center for Youth Studies, 1986

people—boys and girls, young lives created in the image of God, precious souls for whom Christ died. And they surround us. This "mission field" includes our homes, schools, hang-outs, stores, factories, restaurants, offices, churches, parks, and neighborhoods.

Ministry to junior- and senior-high-age young people is crucial because they are at a crossroads, a decision point. They ask tough questions; they seek honest answers. And high school provides us with the last chance for touching a total cross-section of the community; it is the last time a generation is together. After graduation, the class splits . . . forever.

At the same time, adolescence may be the first time a "child" can make mature decisions. Because values are being tested and established, adolescence is the right time to introduce young people to Christ.

The problem is that there is a great gap between the death of Christ for them and the modern teenager, between their lives and the Good News. People are needed to stand in this gap, to hold in one hand the hand of the Lord Jesus and in the other the hand of the young person for whom He died. That's called evangelism.

Who will:
- give love to those who are hurting?
- offer help to the desperate?
- bring hope to the despairing?
- share Christ with the lost?

For too long we have hired professionals to do the job—pastors, Christian education directors, Campus Life staff members, and youth ministers. Because of their experience and skill, we expect them to shoulder the load . . . winning youth for Christ. Their work is important, but it is not enough. To begin to touch the lives of the young people in our world will take an army of caring Christians—parents reaching their children and their children's friends, adults reaching neighborhood kids, teenagers reaching their peers.

The requirements for service in this evangelism "corps" are few—genuine commitment to Christ as Saviour and Lord, deep concern for youth, and a willingness to spend time with them. Age is no barrier—young person, adult, parent, grandparent . . . nor is occupation—secretary, minister, janitor, dentist, housewife.

Do you qualify for this much-needed army? Do you have:
- a commitment to Christ?
- a concern for youth?
- a willingness to spend time?

If you can answer yes to those questions, this book is for you. It has been written to motivate and mobilize you to reach young people for Christ.

CHAPTER TWO

Clutter in the Marketplace

My phone rang. Instinctively I put down my book and hurried to answer it.

"Hello, Mr. Veerman?"

"Yes."

"Are you interested in improving your investments?"

"Well—"

"Our company is making a special offer to you (pause), Mr. Veerman. A representative will be in your neighborhood in the next few days and—"

"No thank you!"

Without waiting for the details of this latest phone offer, I slammed down the receiver and returned to my chair. With a steady stream of such calls, I figured I had heard it all before, and I had better things to do. Of course that person could have saved me money or enriched my life. It's doubtful, but I'll never know.

A few years ago, a computer salesman shared his experience with me. He had just started to work for I.B.M. Convinced that he had a superior product to sell—a software package for small businesses—and confident of his sales ability, he enthusiastically made his calls. But he couldn't get through the door. To most of his potential customers and their secretaries, he was just one of a host of computer salesmen with similar claims. *Their* products were also guaranteed to revolutionize the company's efficiency and productivity. Computers were inundating America with a myriad of manufacturers, sellers, and middlemen. Their claims splashed across the media, with obvious and subtle inducements to buy: incentives, discounts, state of the art technology, applications. These businessmen and women were suffering from computer phobia or data overload, or else they said they already had adequate systems and were sure they needed nothing else. Certainly they didn't need to hear the spiel of another salesman, they thought.

The problem? There was "clutter in the marketplace." In other words, the clamor of a multitude of competing products and claims became, in essence, an unbearable noise, closing

---

RELIGION AND THE MEDIA

Religious Radio Stations	1,370
Religious TV Stations	221
Organizations Producing Radio Programs	596
Organizations Producing TV Programs	414
Religious Radio Programs	807
Religious TV Programs	1,061

Information for 1987, from National Religious Broadcasters

the ears and minds of potential customers. With doors slamming shut all over his territory, my friend soon learned that if he were going to be successful in sales, he would have to design a new approach, a way to stand out from the crowd, to break through the clutter. And he did.

The strategy was simple—he would service his present customers to the best of his ability. He would become personally involved with them, their company, and their needs. The product and his service would produce satisfied customers, models, real-life examples of what the software could do. They would be living affirmations of his sales claims. This salesman succeeded where others failed because he broke through the clutter. People saw the difference in their associates and competitors; they heard about what the product was doing; and they wanted to know more. His personal involvement got his "foot in the door."

But there is clutter of another type. Check out your TV and radio listings. Most major markets have one Christian television station and at least two Christian radio stations. In addition, many religious broadcasters purchase time on other channels. And most call-in shows can't go long without discussing "higher powers" and personal beliefs. Add to this the multitudes of "off brand" religions and cults vying for a following. Then turn to the church section in your phone book or newspaper and count the number of houses of worship advertising their claims and benefits. Religious "outlets" abound.

In the last two decades, we've seen an avalanche of Chris-

Total number of religious titles sold through *Christian* bookstores in 1985	39,390,000
Total number of books published annually (Christian and secular)	53–55,000

Information for 1985, from Christian Booksellers' Association

tian music, Christian books, and big-name Christian personalities—speakers, politicians, athletes, and others. Religion has become high profile and big business. In governmental halls and hearings, religious issues are discussed with regularity. Prayer in schools, evolution, secular humanism, and abortion have become political footballs. And, when would-be spiritual leaders fall from grace, news of their sexual and financial scandals overflows into prime time, with charges, counter-charges, claims, and condemnations.

There's clutter in the marketplace.

Despite the negative publicity, with all this Gospel visibility, many Christians assume that the tide has turned, that the message of Christ is being heard and accepted by many more than ever before, and that all they have to do is send a few

---

CLEARING OUT DEBRIS

One often has to listen to a lot of perversions of the Gospel and clear away a lot of debris before being able to lay out the real Gospel. A man once spent half an hour telling me about the faith as he understood it from a relative, who was some sort of religious fanatic.

After he had finished, I said, "I'm glad you told me about the God you don't believe in, because I don't believe in that God either." Then I began to tell him the Gospel message about a God who loves us so much He came to earth and experienced life among us in the person of Jesus Christ, going to the cross to take care of our sins.

When I had finished, the man said he didn't realize it was that way. He thought God was up there just waiting to zap us for being bad.

Jay Kesler from *Practical Christianity* (Wheaton, Ill.: Tyndale House Publishers, 1987).

dollars to their favorite evangelists, and, before long, the world will be reached.

I wish it were that simple but, unfortunately, the opposite is true. All the media evangelists and other Christian voices seem to be just an annoying din to the average person, the "man on the street." Like my experience with the telephone salesman, mentally they hang up the phone or slam the door. And the gulf is widening between non-Christians and Christians. If you were to take an informal poll of the religious attitudes and beliefs of your neighbors, for example, I think you would hear answers like these:

● "It doesn't matter what you believe in. All religions are basically the same. What matters is that you are sincere."

● "No, I don't go to church anymore. I used to go as a kid, but we've kinda gotten away from it."

● "Sure I believe in heaven. I figure when I die, I'll get in. I'm not so bad. I've never killed anybody or anything like that. Besides, I believe in a God of love."

● "All those TV evangelists are in it for the money. They sound good—so pious and self-righteous—but what are they really like?"

Most scientific polls confirm these results, finding that contemporary Americans are religious, but their religion hardly affects their lives. They have a warm, nostalgic feeling about God, but they are turned off to organized religion and anything that smacks of theology.

This dethroning of the self-giving God and the enthroning of the self-seeking self as God is psychologically devastating. The head of a sorority of a university said to me: "Ours is an uncommitted generation—committed only to ourselves. The next generation will be committed to a mental institution."

E. Stanley Jones, from *A Song of Ascents* (Nashville: Abingdon, 1968).

LOST IN AMERICA

Not only are there more unreached, lost, unsaved people than ever, but also in our increasingly secular society they are further away from truth than ever.

Consider my neighborhood—a classic middle-class, suburban subdivision. During the summer, children ride bikes in the streets, and mothers stroll on sidewalks which border neatly manicured lawns, pushing baby carriages or walking their dogs. Saturdays come alive with the hum of lawnmowers, edgers, and power rakes. We have block parties, a pool, a community organization, and neighborhood watch. Most of the homes consist of a family with two parents. They're good people, with decent values—honest, hardworking, and desiring to be good parents and citizens. Our city is filled with churches. In fact, recently *every* school in town had a church meeting in it on Sunday. It would be easy to imagine much more difficult or hardened mission fields.

But it's a secular society. Many of my neighborhood friends have only a memory of church. And their children have even less.

When we moved here, Kara, my eldest daughter, made friends quickly with girls in the surrounding blocks. Eventually she invited one of them to come to church with us. When she accepted the invitation, Amy asked what she should wear and how she should act. She had never been to church before.

A few years ago, I joined with other parents to organize and run a Campus Life/JV club, Youth for Christ's program for junior highers. The meetings feature fun, teaching, and brief talks about Christ. One of the activities involved a short quiz, which included the question, "What have we been talking about for the last few weeks?" Thinking that the answer had something to do with our talks, Kristy called across the room to a friend, "How do you spell 'Jesus'?"

Those kids were biblically illiterate. They had heard of Christ, but they didn't even know how to spell His name.

THE GROWTH OF YOUTH MINISTRIES

At the end of the Second World War, American streets were filled with servicemen, and young people seemed to be every-

---

KIDS AND TV

Current studies show that the TV set is turned on in U.S. homes an average of 7 hours per day. . . . By the end of high school, malleable young people have seen an average of 350,000 commercials. That is the equivalent of 1½ years of 8-hour work days.

from *Who Speaks For God?* by Charles Colson (Nashville: Thomas Nelson, 1985).

---

where. Sensing God's call, men and women of vision decided to focus their ministries on this new generation. At that time very few evangelical churches or denominations had full-time youth workers, so these ministers sailed uncharted seas. Some chose to work within local churches. Some, like young pastors Torrey Johnson and Jim Rayburn, organized those of similar commitment for the mission. From their efforts sprang Youth for Christ and Young Life. Known as "para-church" organizations, these and others carried the torch of youth ministry. In the succeeding years, churches across the country hired staff members who were specialists in communicating with young people to run youth groups, and Christian colleges and seminaries added youth ministry to their curriculums. Today, large churches host weekly meetings with hundreds of kids, and even small congregations have youth groups.

This emphasis on youth ministry also forced Christian publishing houses to develop appropriate Sunday School and youth group materials. Scripture Press, Gospel Light, Christian Endeavor, David C. Cook, and others responded. This movement also spawned a host of new publishers and youth resources, among them *Campus Life* magazine, *Group* magazine, Youth Specialities, Camfel Productions, Motivational Media, Son Life, Teen Vision, and many others.

In many ways it can be said that youth ministry has never

been so effective or far-reaching. Church youth groups feature creative, entertaining, and interesting programs; scores of musicians, comedians, and speakers provide concerts and rallies; and the resource catalog overflows with videos, tapes, films, and ideas. I'm afraid, however, that most of these efforts are "preaching to the choir"—efforts expended on those who are already evangelized. In the past few decades, we have focused attention on our own needs, making sure that *our* children are surrounded by everything that is Christian. In the process, we have isolated ourselves from those who need us and who need the Gospel.

After our local Campus Life/JV club got off the ground, we were approached by a woman who had a similar vision for her neighborhood. About twenty parents representing a half-dozen churches came to a meeting she organized, and a local Youth for Christ staff person and I explained the purpose of the program—to reach non-Christian junior highers for Christ. Later I called the woman to see how the parents had responded. With deep disappointment she explained that they had decided not to get involved. Instead, most of them had decided to sponsor a weekly Bible study for their own kids. They really weren't that interested in reaching out to others.

"I was happy and complacent in my youth ministry, rocking along with 125 junior high students, breaking attendance records week after week. Nobody in the city could touch my program or my numbers. What a year!

Then I blew it! I committed youth pastor suicide. I walked onto a junior high campus . . . and then another, and then another. I was confronted with reality: In my city, over 45,000 junior high students never attended a church—on any basis, regular or otherwise!"

Mark Gold, from "Evangelism," *Working With Youth* (Wheaton, Ill.: Victor Books, 1982.)

REACHING THE UNREACHED

Youth for Christ, Young Life, and other groups still focus on the unchurched, but the audience of unreached young people is vast. Take the typical public high school as an example. In a school of 2,000, it would be quite generous to say that 500 students are actively involved in any evangelical Christian youth group. But even if this were true, if that many were involved, there still would be 1,500 young people outside of a consistent Gospel witness.

At a Campus Life "Leadership Breakfast," one young man responded to the speaker by writing on his react card, "Help." I knew this young man, Kevin, from school; he was the student body president. I gave him a call, and we got together over a Coke. I learned that he had no religious background whatsoever. His father had been under the influence of a Roman Catholic grandmother who was always dragging him to mass, so Kevin's father had determined to avoid church at all costs. Kevin's mother didn't care either way, so he was raised in a thoroughly secular home. But Kevin was

---

Dr. Win Arn and his son, Charles, have polled 14,000 lay people about who and what was responsible for their coming to Christ. Here are the eye-opening results of their study:

Special need (of individual)	1–2%
Walk-in (to church)	2–3%
Pastor	5–6%
Visitation	1–2%
Sunday School	4–5%
Church program	2–3%
Evangelistic campaign	5%
Friends/relatives	75–90%

Dr. Win Arn, founder and president of the Institute for American Church Growth

empty inside, and something our speaker said about knowing God had caught his attention.

We met many times over the following weeks and months. Kevin's sharp mind probed and pushed, and his questions seemed endless. But he listened carefully and devoured anything I gave him to read. Eventually, Kevin gave his life to Christ.

BREAKING THROUGH

As people committed to Jesus Christ and to spreading His Word, we must break out of our cloisters to reach these young people. They are far from church, but they are close to us.

A common strategy is to rent an auditorium, print and post flyers and posters, and bring in skilled musicians and a speaker. There is a place for these professionals. They are skilled at their craft and can communicate effectively. But the very nature of the religious clutter renders that approach lifeless.

Another suggestion would be to spread the word through Christian videos or records. Stryper, Amy Grant, and other Christian artists have made inroads into the secular music world and are often featured on rock stations or MTV. Certainly their efforts are laudable, and they provide a refreshing alternative to immoral rock stars, videos, and records. But television sets, radios, and videotapes are impersonal tools. Someone must still interpret the message and fill in the blanks.

I'm sure that fertile imaginations will invent other "creative" communication efforts—Gospel letters, comic strips, megaphones, skywriting—all of which add to the clutter.

The answer to the problem of clutter in the religious marketplace does not lie with paper or programs. The only way to break through to people is with *people*—building relationships, becoming personally involved in lives, just as our salesman friend did by selling software along with personal service.

There are no shortcuts. Relationships take time to establish and to develop. I had to spend many hours over nearly a year with Kevin. He got to know me, and then heard the message. Only through our personal involvement with young people will they take time to listen to our words and accept our Lord.

AN OPEN LETTER

Dear Christians,

I have been authorized by God to give you this message. You are to go to all people everywhere and call them to become My disciples. You are to baptize them and teach them to obey all that I have commanded you.

Don't forget, I will be with you always to help you, even to the end of the world. I will never forsake you because I love you. Please don't forsake Me.

With all My love, Jesus Christ

Dear Jesus Christ,

We acknowledge the receipt of Your memo.

Your proposal is both interesting and challenging; however, due to a shortage of personnel, as well as several other financial and personal obligations, we do not feel that we can give proper emphasis to Your challenge at this time.

A committee has been appointed to study the plan and its feasibility. We should have a report to bring to our congregation sometime in the future. You may rest assured that we will give this our careful consideration, and our board will think about it for some future action.

We appreciate Your offer to serve as a resource Person, and should we care to undertake this project sometime later, we will be in contact.

Cordially, The Christians

From YFC Ministry Resource Manual 5

CHAPTER THREE

"Yes, But..."

As a student in a Christian college, I had been active in youth ministry, singing in large rallies, performing skits for church youth groups, and speaking for Bible clubs. I knew that God was calling me to this ministry full-time, and so I made plans for seminary and for working with the local Youth for Christ chapter. In discussing my plans with the YFC executive director, however, I learned that his idea of ministry differed significantly from mine. I was used to meetings, planning them and performing in them; he wanted me to focus on personal relationships, getting to know kids and establishing friendships with them. I was used to young people coming to my programs to hear me; he wanted me to go into their world, to meet them.

Suddenly my past experience and training seemed irrelevant, and I felt totally inadequate for the task. He wanted me to go to high school campuses and hangouts, to spend at least ten hours a week with kids for each school in my charge. I wasn't sure where to go or what to do when I got there. I wondered how to dress, what to say, and even how to stand.

Nervously I approached the school and walked in the front door. Greeted by empty halls, I breathed a sigh of relief and slowly began to investigate. I discovered the office, the gymnasium, the library, and a dozen classrooms in between, noting the similarities and differences between this building and my old high school. Suddenly the passing bell brought me back to reality, and I was quickly engulfed by teenage bodies, caught in a human traffic jam. As kids hurried to their classes, I tried to smile confidently and even managed a few feeble hellos, but the faces became a blur as they passed. Minutes later, the halls emptied and were silent save for the muffled voices of teachers and the rhythmic click of my heels as I walked to the exit.

After school that day, I visited football practice. From the safety of the sidelines near the team trainer, I watched the scrimmage, hoping that kids would see me and know that I was interested in them (or at least that eventually they would connect me with Campus Life). The coaches probably wondered who I was—a new student? An older brother of a player? A scout from the opposition? But the players didn't seem to notice, clawing and sweating through two hours of whistles, yells, and colliding bodies. One lonely hour later, I walked back to my car with only dusty shoes and self-doubts to show for my first day "on the job" in personal youth ministry. While driving to my apartment, I wondered what good I had done and how I would ever break through to this foreign world of high schoolers.

Since then, I have learned much about how to meet kids, and I have become convinced of the necessity for entering their domain. But it hasn't gotten a whole lot easier. After more than 25 years of youth work, certain fears continue to surface, and new excuses enter my mind. I still go there, however, because I know it works; I have seen God work through me. And I know that there is no substitute for *personal* involvement in the lives of individuals. It is the only way to break through the clutter and to win the right to be heard.

SOWING THE SEEDS

I went fishing with a youth worker one day and asked him why more lay people don't witness to their faith. He thought about that for a little bit and then said, "Maybe it's because they think they have to convert people, and they're afraid they're going to fail."

It's our business to sow the seeds, not to harvest the grain. We don't have to worry about failure when we sow. A farmer doesn't sow one seed for every plant he wants. He sows thousands of seeds because he knows not every seed will grow into a plant. Sowing is vitally important—if the seeds aren't sown, there won't be any plants. Our job is to sow the seed. We can let God worry about the harvest.

Oswald Hoffman from *Practical Christianity* (Wheaton, Ill.: Tyndale House Publishers, 1987).

OVERCOMING FEAR

Fear is a natural response to anything new or foreign, especially when egos are on the line. I was never *physically* afraid of adolescents (that is, afraid for my personal safety); rather my fears were more *emotionally* or psychologically based. I was afraid of what the teenagers would think of me. After all, they might ridicule or insult "this guy who always hangs around." I also feared the unknown, being in a situation where I was uncomfortable, not knowing what to do or say, and not being in control. And, to be totally honest, many of my feelings related to my past experience; I felt threatened by the types of students who rejected *me* when I was in high school.

There are other bases for fear. A few decades ago, we heard of the "generation gap"—the lack of understanding between adults and adolescents, parents and teenagers, administration and students. This "gap" exists and is widened with the development of the youth culture and their unique pressures and problems. Kids seem to live in their own world with their own language, dress, and social mores. And when we hear or read of teenage exploits in vandalism, sex, and gangs, the gap seems to be an insurmountable gulf.

Because of these fear factors, most adults limit their contacts with junior or senior high schoolers, usually avoiding them with the exception of their children, baby-sitters, or fast-food employees. So when asked to teach, sponsor, or chaperone, they find convenient excuses not to become involved.

But this book is all about getting involved with young people, and its purpose is to motivate and train adults to enter their world, and to reach and touch them for Christ. The fears are natural, but we dare not allow fear to paralyze us, to keep us from this ministry.

What are your reservations, those perceived barriers to your involvement? And what are your excuses, the reasons you give for not reaching out? Here are some of those which I have thought, felt, and heard over the years.

ELIMINATING EXCUSES

Excuse #1—"I don't know any young people." This is a common response, and the answer is simply, "take another look!" The world is filled with kids and a lot of them are probably in your world. Think of your neighborhood or your church. Or what about the kids where you get your car washed or at McDonald's? And then there's that group that hangs around in the park.

A few years ago, when I considered buying a mini-van, I began to see mini-vans everywhere. It seemed as though everyone had one. Because I was thinking about that type of automobile, I became sensitive to their presence. They had been there all the time, but I hadn't seen them because I wasn't looking.

Take another look around you, and list the teenagers who touch your life. You'll be surprised at how many you know.

Excuse #2—"I'm not the 'youth leader' type." This statement implies that there is an ideal youth leader: he or she is young, attractive, athletic, outgoing, multi-talented, confident, intelligent, and articulate. The truth is that very few of those

---

EXCUSES

Moses said, "Oh, come on now! Be sensible! Not me! I'm a terrible speaker. They'd never listen to me." And God said, "Oh, for crying out loud! OK, I'll send your brother to help with the speaking." And Moses led God's people out of disintegration.

Jonah said, "Oh, come on now! Be sensible! Not me! I'm not the type." And after a rather unexpected vacation in a fish, just thinking things over, he talked to the Ninevites and led them God's way.

And Zacharias said, "Oh, come on now! Be sensible! Not me! My wife and I are too old to have any kids." And God said, "Oh, shut up!" And he did shut up—for nine months. And John was born, and the way for Christ opened up.

And I heard a child say, "I can't serve God; I'm too young."

And I heard a boy say, "I can't serve God; I'm not good enough."

And I heard a woman say, "I can't serve God; I'm not skilled enough."

I wonder if God ever gets any new problems.

From *God Is No Fool*, by Lois Cheney (Nashville: Abingdon, 1969).

"superstars" exist. Most people are a blend of strengths and weaknesses, and God uses both to reach others. Instead of natural ability or charisma, God is looking for availability—willingness to pray for the lost, to love others, and to go where He sends us.

Think about the Christian adults who made an impact on your life. What were they like? I remember Sunday School teachers—a woman in her sixties, a man with a crippled leg, and a television repairman. None of them played football with me, but I knew they cared. I also had a pastor who listened to me and respected my ideas, even when they bordered on heresy. As a Youth for Christ executive director, I have hired and supervised scores of professional youth workers. They come in all shapes and sizes. Often the "most gifted" are the least effective, and the "low profile" ones turn out to be winners. Take another look at yourself—with a fresh perspective on what is really needed, you may begin to see yourself as the "youth worker type."

Excuse #3—"Youth work is a job for professionals." The answer to this is "yes and no." Yes, there is a tremendous need for men and women trained in youth work who are committed to serving God in this ministry full-time and who see it as a career; but, as stated in chapter 1, this is not enough. Reaching a generation of young people will take the combined efforts of concerned Christian adults, youth workers of every kind—full-time, part-time, and volunteer. Consider the church in the first century or in poor countries today. There are full-time Christian workers, but lay people carry the bulk of the ministry. The idea that we can "hire" someone to do everything for us is a materialistic response to a very spiritual need.

Excuse #4—"My 'little bit' won't mean much." In the face of the tidal wave of problems in the vast sea of unreached youth, it is easy to feel as though our small contribution is insignificant. But take another look at young people, from God's perspective. Each person is of infinite value to Him. You may be the difference in the life of just a few young people, but your impact will have eternal consequences. And there is also the principle of multiplication. Each one of those new believers can reach others who will reach others. Your life and witness can have staggering implications.

Our excuses may simply be another name for *fear*. Perhaps you have voiced (or thought about) other "reasons" for avoiding adolescents. Instead of making excuses, try to focus on the power and love of God and remember the great need that exists.

In addition to excuses, however, there are barriers which must be overcome—real factors which could limit our effectiveness.

WHERE TO START

"But, Lord, You know that I'm nearly 30 years old—what can I do?" "But, Lord, You know I'm nearly 40—do you have a place for me?"

God is saying, "You are finally worth trusting to some young person."

"Lord, You know I am single. What can I do?"

God is saying, "You have the resources and the time to give, and I will bless them."

"Lord, You know my wife and I have no children, and we don't know how to work with kids."

God says, "You will have My children and I will teach you."

You and I live in a strategic time in eternity right now. Picture an hourglass. The sand represents our entire culture, and the bottleneck represents the high school—the institution virtually every young person in our culture will pass through. We stand at the bottleneck, where we have the opportunity to help fulfill the Great Commission. The student must pass by you. Will you reach out?

Bill Stewart in *Discipling the Young Person*, Paul Fleischmann, editor (San Bernardino, Calif.: Here's Life Publishers, Inc., 1985).

BREAKING DOWN BARRIERS

Barrier #1—Age. The generation gap is real, and it begins immediately upon graduation from high school. From that day on, kids seem younger, "different," and hard to understand. As we age, the gap widens, and we wonder if anyone can relate to kids today. Add to this the idea that "young" people can relate better to "younger" youth workers, and age is a barrier between us and youth ministry.

Of course, a good case can be built for young youth workers. They still remember vividly what junior high and high school were like and can make specific references in conversation, counseling, and teaching. In addition, they have a tremendous reservoir of energy, enabling them to hike, climb, bike, run, swim, and stay up all night with kids. If they are unmarried, they can maintain a flexible schedule and allow for spontaneous talks, trips, or outings.

Youthful youth workers have a lot going for them, but so do older adults. And I speak as one having seen both sides.

After college, I attacked my new ministry with vigor, spending long hours with kids, trying just about any type of program that would work. As the years passed, however, I began to question how long I would last in this type of ministry. Would I lose touch with kids, could I continue to run at their pace, and would they "turn me off" because of my age?

But as I matured and changed, my ministry "deepened." No, I didn't last as long in marathon basketball games, but I found that my ministry remained as effective and rewarding as ever. As I got older, each of my life experiences (marriage, fatherhood, aging, physical problems, and others) provided rich ministry resources. I remember talking with a high school senior who kept complaining that her mother just didn't understand her. After asking how old her parents were, I calmly shared that I was older. I was then able to explain what they might be feeling and experiencing as parents of a teenager.

Barrier #2—Time. Everyone is busy, frantically rushing through life meeting the demands of family, work, and other interests. We even work at our leisure time. On a recent trip, Gail caught me muttering about the traffic and pressuring the whole family to move quickly to meet our schedule. She reminded me that our vacation started at the driveway, not at the destination. But that's how we live, isn't it? With all of these pressures on us, it's difficult to imagine carving out any hours to be with kids or to go to their activities.

This is not an easy barrier to overcome if we only consider the issue of the availability of time. It really is a question of values and priorities. In other words, if you have a deep desire to see young people come to Christ and if you believe that reaching them is *very important,* you will order your priorities and organize your schedule accordingly. If, however, you mean only to give lip service to youth ministry, you probably

---

GOOD SAMARITAN

A class of seminary students was assigned a sermon on the Good Samaritan. They spent weeks studying the Scripture and commentaries to prepare their messages about a Samaritan who had helped a man who had been beaten, robbed, and left to die. What they didn't know was that the professors "planted" a man along the path they would take to the lecture hall, and made up the man to appear to be beaten, robbed, and left to die. One at a time, they came to deliver their sermons, and one by one, they all walked around the man on the sidewalk. All of them flunked the exam that day, because the test was not to see if they knew the story or could communicate the story, but whether or not they would put into practice what Jesus was teaching.

From YFC Ministry Resource Manual 5

---

won't find time for it.

On the other hand, your part in reaching young people does not have to mean a massive time commitment. There are all sorts of ways to become involved with kids, using one's talents, interests, and regular routine. We will discuss these in succeeding chapters.

Barrier #3—Lack of understanding of youth needs and culture. This is a legitimate concern, but it can be overcome. Research organizations exist to provide all the information you will ever need—"facts" about the lifestyle, fads, and opinions of typical young people and trends in their society. But your own informal research may prove to be more helpful. Go to a few high school football games, read some of the popular teen magazines, watch their favorite TV shows, visit a local record store, and listen to the top "rock" station. You'll soon be an "expert." Even without all this knowledge, you can impact young lives, just by being you and by being available.

Barrier #4—Lack of ministry skills. This barrier includes knowing how to meet young people, how to build relationships with them, and how to share the Gospel with them. It also is a valid concern. One of the purposes of this book, however, is to teach you how to reach young people for Christ. Read on.

ADVANTAGES ON YOUR SIDE

Despite the fears and the barriers which must be overcome by the mature volunteer youth worker, there are some automatic advantages to being an adult working with young people in ministry.

The first thing you have going for you is *maturity and stability.* Through commitments and experiences on their jobs, in their communities, and in their families, adults have learned to be responsible—to manage themselves and their time. They know their gifts, abilities, and life priorities. They are reliable, punctual, and not susceptible to the wide swings of youthful emotions. In a world of shifting values, fallen heros, and rampant untruths, young people need someone on whom they can rely, who will be there during the tough times—someone who will accept them as they are. That someone can be you.

You also have the advantage of *patience and commitment.* Anyone who has been through the difficult early years of marriage or of raising a family has learned patience. Older workers have seen it all, including the setbacks and failures of

---

THE UNCOMMITTED GENERATION

"This generation, or at the most the next, must decide between materialistic, atheistic Communism and the kingdom of God on earth."

E. Stanley Jones, *A Song of Ascents* (Nashville: Abingdon, 1968).

people of all ages. These leaders will not push young people to meet their personal needs and will understand when teenagers "act their age." They also know that discipleship is a lifetime process, one that does not end at age 18.

In an era when the family is under attack, young people need to see living proof that truly Christian marriages exist and that parents can live for Christ and love their families. Youth ministers who spend hours with the young people in their worlds, and then open their homes and lives to those same kids, make a tremendous impact in the area of a *family model*. There is no substitute for a life-sized example of the lordship of Christ.

With age comes experience. A person who has borne a child, undergone surgery, buried a loved one, and survived financial crises has a *wealth of content* to share. Bible studies come alive with real examples. Young people have the misconception that pain is the exception in life. Having experienced more pain, older adults know better, offer a wider perspective, and can balance idealism with reality.

Another advantage you have to use in your outreach to kids concerns your *connections*. Those who have lived and worked in a community for any length of time know their way around. With an informal network of friends and associates, they know who to call for counsel, employment, or tickets to the big game. They can put kids in touch with others who can help them.

To have an effective ministry with young people, a person must know how to relate to adults. Teens are surrounded by adults—parents, neighbors, teachers, coaches, employers—and cannot be isolated from them. The person who has lived and worked in this adult world will understand the older generation and will be trusted. He or she will not be seen as the "college kid with the crazy ideas," a possible drug pusher, or a cult leader. You can tap into your *rapport with* adults in your ministry.

Older leaders are less likely to be the object of "crushes" and, hopefully, far removed from personal romantic ideas and sexual temptations. It still is advisable to work with kids of the same sex, but even in opposite sex ministry, fewer of those

---

BONDAGE

Harry Houdini, the famed escape artist, issued a challenge wherever he went. He could be locked in any jail cell in the country, he claimed, and set himself free in short order. Always he kept his promise, but one time something went wrong.

Houdini entered the jail in his street clothes; the heavy, metal doors clanged shut behind him. He took from his belt a concealed piece of metal, strong and flexible. He set to work immediately, but something seemed to be unusual about this lock. For thirty minutes he worked and got nowhere. An hour passed, and still he had not opened the door. By now he was bathed in sweat and panting in exasperation, but he still could not pick the lock.

Finally, after laboring for two hours, Harry Houdini collapsed in frustration and failure against the door he could not unlock. But when he fell against the door, it swung open! *It had never been locked at all!* But *in his mind* it was locked, and that was all it took to keep him from opening the door and walking out of the jail cell.

From *Parables, Etc.*, June 1983. Reprinted in YFC Ministry Resource Manual 5

---

other problems will arise.

In addition, being a volunteer means that the person's motives are genuine love and concern. He or she has nothing to sell, it's not a "job," and there's no money in it. Kids are impressed with those who help because they care.

Coming face-to-face with young people can elicit a myriad of mixed feelings and fears. In addition, there are some very real barriers which must be overcome if adults are to have an effective ministry with the younger generation. Despite these limitations, adult volunteers bring great strengths to the ministry, including stability, maturity, commitment, patience, and knowledge. And in the midst of the ministry are God's promises—He will be with us (Hebrews 13:5), He will work in us (Philippians 2:13), and He will speak through us (2 Corinthians 5:20).

CHAPTER FOUR

Principles and Power

Imagine that you are a journalist, interviewing people in a downtown shopping and business district. Pacing the sidewalks and storefronts with recorder in hand, you ask each person one question: "What is an evangelist?" What do they say? What would you say?

The word evangelist evokes many images in society, most of them negative or fanatical. Even Christians have mental images of stereotypical evangelists. We may think of someone speaking to a packed stadium, a man leaning over a television pulpit, a young person shouting on a street corner, a professional athlete sharing her testimony, or intense men and women pushing leaflets at commuters. These people may be evangelists, but evangelism is much broader than those mental images. In reality, an "evangelist" is someone who communicates the Gospel, the Good News about Christ.

One of the Apostle Paul's last statements to Timothy, his

young protégé, was to "do the work of an evangelist" (2 Timothy 4:5). This was centuries before the printing press, microphones, and electronic media. Timothy was charged with the responsibility of telling others about Christ. That is our task as well . . . and that is evangelism.

APPROACHES

The "evangelism umbrella" covers a multitude of styles, approaches, and techniques, everything from television super-preachers to those who display Bible banners at major sporting events. When asked to "evangelize," many picture the caricatures mentioned above and envision thrusting a tract into a reluctant hand at the airport, knocking door-to-door like an overaggressive salesman or cult follower, or preaching on a corner in skid row. No wonder most people hesitate to get involved.

Of course much of what is labeled "evangelism," isn't. Far from the New Testament examples, today's version of evangelism has arisen from our culture, church environment, or misguided imaginations. We must refuse to carry these ideas, concepts, or notions into a ministry with young people because they can only damage young lives or forever turn them off to the Gospel.

Some have been taught, for example, that effectiveness of evangelism is measured solely by statistics with the most important question being, "How many decisions did we have?" These individuals come from an environment where the measure of a speaker's success was how many "came forward" or were counseled or signed cards.

Others equate evangelism with long public invitations or altar calls, exerting much emotional and psychological pressure to get a response.

Still others believe that the only way to reach people for Christ is to "buttonhole" them—running up to any stranger, grabbing him, dropping the "Gospel bomb," asking him if he knows the Lord (is ready to die/is born-again), giving him a few minutes to hear the spiel and to respond one way or the other, checking him off as a "yes" or "no," and then leaving.

There is another approach which is almost the opposite.

Rejecting pressure tactics and the wild-eyed, fanatic image, these "evangelists" use a cooler form. Emphasizing that one's lifestyle can mirror faith, they seldom confront anyone with his or her need. The message is watered down to "God is great, God is good" . . . and few, if any, come to Christ.

None of these approaches can rightly be called biblical. But if we would effectively and responsibly carry God's message to young people, we must begin by understanding what His Word teaches by precept and illustration—the New Testament principles of evangelism. The six principles which follow are based on materials developed by Ron Hutchcraft.

SIX PRINCIPLES OF RESPONSIBLE EVANGELISM
Principal #1—Maximum Influence
Jesus said, "You are the light of the world. A city on a hill cannot be hidden. Neither do people light a lamp and put it under a bowl. Instead they put it on its stand, and it gives light to everyone in the house. In the same way, let your light shine before men, that they may see your good deeds and praise your Father in heaven" (Matthew 5:14-16).

If you come within twenty or thirty miles of Chicago, regardless of the direction, you will see the city. There it sits with the Sears Tower and the rest of the skyline. People have a variety of feelings about Chicago. Some hate it. Some love it. Others are neutral about it. But one thing is sure; you can't ignore it. There sits the city, looming before you, dominating everything. And it's not even on a hill.

Jesus said that His Gospel and His people should be unignorable. Wherever they are, they should be talked about. They are to penetrate every level of society and be the most noticeable things around. And that's the way Jesus approached His world, influencing as many people as He could.

Maximum influence evangelism is finding *the fastest way to influence the most people the most effectively.* Each word in that definition is important. The "fastest way" might be a Gospel blimp, a bumper sticker, or a neon sign near the high school blinking "God loves you." But those methods would not do the job "most effectively." We must constantly use our sanctified creativity to imagine and plan more effective ways to share Christ with others.

Jesus began by choosing twelve disciples from all kinds of interest groups. Some could influence rich people, others poor; some talked loudly, some softly; some were political revolutionaries, some had "sold out" to the political power structure.

Throughout the Book of Acts we see God touching many people who were strategically placed to get the Word out quickly. In Acts 8 there is the Ethiopian dignitary, the queen's treasurer. There is no record of any of the twelve disciples going to Ethiopia, but there is much first-century evidence that Christianity thrived there. In Acts 9 we can see that when God wanted to reach the intellectuals of Greek culture, He touched Saul of Tarsus. In Acts 10, we read that God turned His attention to a Roman military leader, Cornelius. Acts 16 describes the first convert in Europe, Lydia, who was one of the merchants in Philippi. Acts 18 fills us in on one of the first Corinthians to be reached with the Gospel—Crispus, the "chief ruler of the synagogue." In the later chapters we see that Paul entered the courtrooms of Governor Felix, Governor Festus, and King Agrippa. Finally, Paul wrote from prison, "All the saints send you greetings, especially those who belong to Caesar's household" (Philippians 4:22). And so that small group of disciples spread out and began to influence various corners of their world until finally the Gospel walked into Caesar's palace.

Whether by means of media, large meetings, or reaching strategic individuals, many can be exposed to the Gospel through thoughtful, creative, and responsible communication methods.

This principle of maximum influence may not seem to apply directly to your efforts in your home or neighborhood. But don't reject it quickly. There may be special events sponsored by reputable churches or organizations to which you can invite your teenage friends. The musicians and speakers featured at these concerts, activities, or meetings can help bridge the communication gap between you and your guests. And there is the matter of strategic individuals. Think of the potential impact one influential young person can make on his or

---

WORDS AND WITNESSING

Some people say they can't witness because they have a hard time with words. But I've noticed that people who have a hard time with words don't have trouble with all words everywhere. Usually they are comfortable with some friend or family member, and with that person they can talk freely. It's best to forget whether words come hard or easy and major on something entirely different—relationships. It's hard for anybody to walk up to a stranger and begin witnessing. It should be. We need to make friends first, to get close enough to the person so that our witnessing flows out of our concern for him or her. When our relationship is solid, the words will not be difficult.

Calvin Miller from *Practical Christianity* (Wheaton, Ill.: Tyndale House, 1987).

---

her peers. Ask God to lead you to young men and women who can really make a difference in their worlds.

Biblical evangelism involves maximum influence.

Principle #2—Person-centeredness

In John 4 we read about how Jesus began to evangelize in Sychar. He spent time getting through to one woman. And remember that in Luke 15, Jesus said that He would worry more about one lost sheep than ninety-nine safe ones. The same God who believes in maximum influence also believes in approaching one person at a time, making the Good News personal.

"Person-centeredness" means that we operate in the other person's world, not ours. Jesus got through to us by becoming a human being and living on earth among us (John 1:14). He didn't drop the message from the sky or shout it with a celestial megaphone. Jesus became a living, breathing human being—the eternal in a finite package. As a man, He got cold, ate food, and even risked catching leprosy. He became like us. The only thing He didn't do was sin. He got so close to sin, however, that a lot of people thought that He had stepped over the line. "He's a drunk," they said. Jesus went to dinner at Matthew's house with a bunch of notorious crooks (Mark 2:15-17), and to Zaccheus' house too (Luke 19:6-10). Jesus' reputation was hurt because of these visits.

Like Jesus, we must invade the world of non-Christian kids if we are to reach them. This means going to their campuses, athletic practices, hangouts, school plays, and other places and activities. We may be misunderstood at times for doing so, but we can't expect teenagers to come looking for us.

Another requirement of person-centeredness is that we speak to the needs of the other person. How would you feel if you went to the doctor with a sore throat and he began to X-ray your arm? Probably you would conclude that the M.D. was a quack or at the least he was out of touch with his patients. The same is true with evangelism. Before applying the Gospel-medicine, we must find out where young people are hurting. They may be struggling with an abusive home, sexual guilt, or an emotional problem. Or they may not be experiencing any symptoms of their "sin-disease."

We cannot assume that non-Christian teenagers understand our technical Christian terminology (e.g., "born again," "sin," "eternal life," "God loves you," etc.). This means that we shouldn't jump in with both feet (often in our mouths) with a memorized presentation or personal testimony. Instead, we must respect each person as a unique individual and treat him or her with loving care. We want to see healing take place, not just administer a certain number of shots.

When we are person-centered, we begin at the other person's starting point. Paul wrote, "To the Jews I became like a Jew, to win the Jews. To those under the Law I became like one under the Law (though I myself am not under the Law), so as to win those under the Law. To those not having the Law I became like one not having the Law (though I am not free from God's Law but am under Christ's law), so as to win those not having the law. To the weak I became weak, to win

RELATIONSHIP BUILDING

You and I know that what gets through in the long run with the Gospel is relationships. *Build relationships.* I run into people from my past whom I've worked with and trained and helped and struggled with—and those relationships are absolutely incredible. You will run into those students years and years later. One caution: build relationships, not a subculture. We don't want to build a Christian ghetto. We don't want our students to remove themselves from the culture. We want them to understand culture. We want to disciple them and apprentice them into the world so they can deal with their culture.

Wes Hurd, in *Discipling the Young Person*, Paul Fleischmann, editor (San Bernardino, Calif.: Here's Life Publishers, Inc., 1985).

the weak. I have become all things to all men so that by all possible means I might save some" (1 Corinthians 9:20-22).

This passage doesn't sound like the hard-nosed, dogmatic Paul. But it is. The Gospel which Paul preached stayed constant, but his approach changed with every person he met. Our approaches must be adapted to each individual and each situation. And this is where we must be creative, looking for ways to begin and build relationships with young people, designing strategies to touch lives, and providing opportunities for them to respond to Christ.

Teenagers never determine *what* our message should be, but they always determine *how* we say it. There is no one perfect way to communicate the Gospel; that is why a memorized speech won't work. Young people are not "customers," they are *people*. With customers, what matters most is whether or not they buy; their names, feelings, and concerns are usually not that important. But kids are people, valuable creations of God for whom Christ died. After we get to know them as individuals, we may indeed use a "plan of salvation" to explain the Gospel. But by then we will be sure that the person is interested in finding out about Christ.

A young student once asked a Campus Life staff person a very perceptive question: "If I don't accept your Jesus, will you still be my friend?" Person-centeredness keeps on caring, even after rejection. In Gethsemane, Jesus exemplified this principle when He kept showing love to Judas despite the betrayal.

Principle #3—Spirit-led Boldness

First Thessalonians 2:3-6 describes Paul's evangelistic approach: "For the appeal we make does not spring from error or impure motives, nor are we trying to trick you. On the contrary, we speak as men approved by God to be entrusted with the Gospel. We are not trying to please men but God, who tests our hearts. You know we never used flattery, nor did we put on a mask to cover up greed—God is our witness. We were not looking for praise from men, not from you or anyone else."

This approach of Paul's corresponds with the continual use of the word "boldness" in Acts as the early church hit hard and was "not ashamed of the Gospel" (Romans 1:16). Paul wrote that his message seemed to be ridiculous to the Jews who "demand miraculous signs" and to the Greeks who "look for wisdom." Then he says, "but we preach Christ crucified: a stumbling block to Jews and foolishness to Gentiles, but to those whom God has called, both Jews and Greeks, Christ the power of God and the wisdom of God" (1 Corinthians 1:23-24). To paraphrase this statement we could say, "Some young people want a dramatic sign or emotional experience. Then they say they'll believe in Christ. Others want a different approach; they want a logical treatise on the existence of God because they're very intellectual. But you know what I do? I don't cater to either one. I tell them that Jesus died for them, and that's all I have to say."

In 1 Corinthians 15:1-4 is Paul's definition of the Gospel; it is that Jesus died and rose again. This message was worth being bold about. Paul was simply following Christ who "taught as one who had authority" (Matthew 7:29).

THE CAMERA'S EYE

We communicate something of what we're like all the time. I often imagine that every person I meet has a tiny camera implanted right behind their forehead, and the batteries never run down. The camera's eye is constantly on. Also just down the corrider from the camera is this great film vault which instantly starts films rolling on the giant screen of the mind at the slightest suggestion. Think about it. If I mention the name of _____ to you, the ole' computer immediately starts the film rolling on that person. You passed him in the hall one day when he was laughing uproariously. You saw him with his arms wrapped around a girl at a party. The film keeps rolling, and all of us draw our impressions about others based on the film we've got in storage.

YFC Ministry Resource Manual 5

This may sound as though we should be "buttonholers" after all, but let's look at the first part of this biblical principle—being Spirit-led.

As we read the Gospels, it is amazing how many people Jesus *didn't* touch. He walked into the Bethesda pool, healed one man, and left. In Jericho, huge crowds wanted to see Him, but He was preoccupied with one blind man named Bartimaeus.

Paul had great plans for conducting a crusade in Bithynia, but "the Spirit of Jesus would not allow them to" (Acts 16:7). Jesus and the disciples were not mindless fanatics trying to convert everyone in sight. They were Spirit-led, and the Holy Spirit didn't lead them to everyone. But the ones He *did* point out got the full dose of the Good News. There was no compromising or watering down of the message; they were bold and unashamed.

In ministering to young people, it will be tempting to pull

our punches as we think, "These inner-city kids are tough; I just can't come on too strong like the storefront preachers . . . " or "These suburban kids are so cool, so sophisticated; I just can't come right out and. . . ." We must not rationalize; no kid should make us back off from the Gospel. God will provide opportunities to share the Gospel. When He does, we must lovingly and clearly give His message.

We must also guard against the following substitutes for presenting the Gospel. They sound good, but they are inadequate by themselves.

• *Student excitement about a program or activity.* Assemblies, concerts, high adventure trips, spectacular events, and special activities can generate enthusiasm and excitement among young people. When we've made a big splash and the "in crowd" at the school is saying that the program is the greatest thing going, we can be tempted into thinking that we have arrived and that the Gospel has been communicated. But excitement and attendance are not enough. They are simply tools for communication. The means are not the end.

• *Rapport with young people.* Meeting kids and establishing friendships with them feels good. It's great to be liked and accepted by this group which so many in our society fear or shun. We must remember, however, that God helps us to build these relationships and win the confidence of young people so that we can present Christ to them. When we fear that a young person might not like us anymore if we come on too strong, we betray Jesus. We will be trading off evangelism to preserve rapport. Friendship is simply not enough.

• *Spiritual generalities.* There are many spiritual principles or statements about God which most people believe—"God is love," "We must not neglect the spiritual side of our lives," and even "Christ died for us." These lines are good and true; we can repeat them without fear of controversy or rejection, but we have to get much more specific. We have to communicate the full-fledged Gospel before we are through. Spiritual generalities are not enough.

Spirit-led boldness does not fear rejection. The ultimate failure in ministry is not for a young person to reject Christ. Many have done so in the past, and many, unfortunately, will in the future. If rejection equals failure, then Jesus failed badly many times. Ultimate failure in evangelism is when we don't give kids anything to reject.

There are two ways to lose the loyalty of young people: (1) saying something, presenting the Gospel, which they decide not to accept, and (2) saying nothing so that they walk away disinterested, having heard nothing new. The first is not failure; it is an inevitability of evangelism. The second is criminal. Remember, however, that the rejection must be a rejection of the Jesus of the New Testament, not a distortion from our poor presentation. If our incompetance caused the rejection, then again we are at fault.

A Christian can be bold if she or he is convinced that God is in the business of bringing Christians and non-Christians together for His glory. We enter this ministry with young people knowing full well that we are not the instruments which God will use to reach *every* student. But He will bring us to some of them. Jesus died to change lives—New Testament evangelism involves Spirit-led boldness.

Principle #4—Multiplication
Paul, sitting in prison, knew that he personally wasn't going to do much more evangelizing. He wrote to Timothy, "And the things you have heard me say in the presence of many witnesses entrust to reliable men who will also be qualified to teach others" (2 Timothy 2:2). Paul was an evangelist; he had led many people to Christ, one by one. But he was also a "multiplier"; he also trained others to evangelize.

There are two approaches to evangelism: addition and multiplication. Addition says, "I will be an evangelist in this neighborhood or at this school. I will set up my imaginary booth, so to speak, and try to run as many kids through it as I can. I will tell them what they need to know, check them off as a yes or a no, and keep the line flowing." A lot of kids could find Christ that way.

But multiplication says, "I will set up my booth and lead a kid to Christ. Then I will spend some time with her to make sure she understands how to run a booth of her own at her school. It will take longer than just telling her how to witness;

PRINCIPLE OF MULTIPLICATION

Considering that the church prior to Pentecost numbered only a few hundred believers, this is an astounding achievement. Probably the Christian community within three decades had multiplied four hundredfold, which represents an annual increase of 22 percent for more than a generation, and the rate of growth continued remarkably high for 300 years. By the beginning of the fourth century, when Constantine was converted to Christianity, the number of disciples may have reached 10 or 12 million, or roughly a tenth of the total population of the Roman Empire.

Such growth cannot be sustained by merely adding the children of Christians to the rolls, nor is it the result of large transfers of membership from other congregations. The early church grew by evangelistic multiplication as witnesses of Christ reproduced their lifestyle in the lives of those about them.

The Master Plan of Discipleship, by Robert E. Coleman (Tappan, N.J.: Fleming H. Revell Co., 1987).

I will show her how witnessing in the New Testament is a by-product of a growing relationship with Christ. I will help her become a disciple."

At the beginning, "teen-to-teen" sharing is less effective. The addition method racks up faster totals. Eventually, however, multiplication catches up and takes the lead.

We must constantly ask how we can be effective in reaching youth for Christ; but we should also be involved in training young people to be evangelists. This is the biblical principle of multiplication.

Principle #5—Long-term Concern
Producing a new life takes time. The Lord is waiting, according to 2 Peter 3:9, "not wanting anyone to perish, but every-

one to come to repentance." God is willing to wait.

This does not mean that God wants us to wait forever to present the Gospel. When He gives us the green light, we must boldly and clearly call young men and women to repentance and faith. But we are to be willing to wait for a response. Sometimes the Holy Spirit takes a long time to work internally; we cannot afford to be impatient.

Another reason for patience is that when considering a whole faith, a new style of life, kids are not impulse buyers. They are too smart and are very familiar with outrageous claims by advertisers and politicians. So when someone says, "You should become a Christian," a typical response is, "Oh, really? Why?" (And the person may be thinking, "Where can I watch you for a while?")

They may think it over for a very long time. If eventually they decide yes, they will be further down the road of Christian maturity than the person who just heard a convincing speaker, jumped up, and headed for the counseling room. The ones who take a little longer often turn out to be the most solid.

This means that we must be committed to ministering with certain young people for the long term. It doesn't mean approaching individuals or groups and hitting them with a one-shot Gospel message. Instead, it means becoming involved in their lives, being available to answer questions and making sure they understand the message. It means being credible and authentic over the long haul, being there when the young person is ready to make his or her decision.

Principle #6—Follow-through Care

Here is where we get down to talking about "fruit that will remain." Paul and Timothy said to the Colossians that "we proclaim Him, admonishing and teaching everyone with all wisdom, so that we may present everyone perfect in Christ" (Colossians 1:28).

The person who has only spiritual dwarfs or stillborns to present to God will be ashamed. The Great Commission asks for more than just going and telling; it also says, "Make disciples." This requires ministry on several levels; Jesus touched at least three of them. He made *disciples* of only twelve men, working intensely night and day with them.

He had a relational ministry with a slightly larger circle: Mary Magdalene, Lazarus, Martha, Mary, the Emmaus people, the seventy. They all knew Him; they had the advantage of personal contact with Him.

And He touched the third group, the masses, in an even more limited way. About all He could do was stand up in front of them and say, "Here's My message; I hope some of you will accept it."

We each have favorite areas of ministry. Some are very good at discipling, and would like to do that all the time and avoid the seed-scattering. Others are good at touching crowds of kids, but they get nervous about one-to-one ministry. But to be responsible evangelists, we must minister on all three levels. And then we must be concerned about working out the new salvation (Philippians 2:12) in the lives of kids who find Christ, following through with care in their lives.

When someone becomes a Christian through our witness, we must help that person become grounded in the faith and move him or her along the path to spiritual maturity. This involves teaching him how to study and apply the Bible, how to pray, how to deal with problems, and how to share his faith with others. It also means introducing him to his brothers and sisters in Christ, getting him involved in a local church.

THE POWER
In His final instructions to the disciples, just before leaving them and returning to heaven, Jesus promised that they would receive power from the Holy Spirit and *then* they would be His witnesses throughout the earth (Acts 1:8). In other words, their effective witnessing for Christ, evangelism, would be a natural by-product of God working in and through them by the Holy Spirit.

This is a most important lesson to learn. In all of our evangelism efforts, we must not rely on our creative programs, imaginative and elaborate plans, or clever lines . . . our own strength. Instead, we must depend on God and draw on the

---

THE POWER OF PRAYER

There is *power* in prayer. Much prayer, much power. No prayer, no power. And particularly for those who are working with young people, prayer is one of the most vital subjects that could ever be addressed.

One of the most tragic errors made by those who work with youth is that they underestimate the tremendous job they have in trying to direct young people to Jesus. Young people are the prize sought after by Satan. Thus, it is no secret that those who teach and work with young people at the church where I pastor are, to my knowledge, the best-equipped people I have.

Dr. E.V. Hill in *Discipling the Young Person*, Paul Fleischmann, editor (San Bernardino, Calif.: Here's Life Publishers, Inc., 1985).

---

power of the Holy Spirit to win others to Christ. This means that everything we do must be saturated with prayer, confessing known sin and keeping the communication channels open, and asking God for sensitivity to the opportunities He presents, for the courage to take advantage of them, and for the words to say. We should ask Him to give us insights and creative ideas. Then we can strategize, plan, and work.

The disciples changed their world for Christ because they were led and empowered by the Holy Spirit.

APPLICATION

This is the overall view of New Testament evangelism. As we understand more about these principles, we must make sure that our ministry conforms to them.

The temptation will be to concentrate on whichever of the six principles happens to be our favorite, to the exclusion of the others. If we like confrontation, we can distort the proper role of boldness. If we are by nature low-pressure, we can intentionally misunderstand long-term concern. As we attempt to reach young people for Christ, we must keep all six

principles in mind and center our methods around them—
maximum influence, person-centeredness, Spirit-led boldness,
multiplication, long-term concern, follow-through care—praying always and working in the power of the Holy Spirit.

CHAPTER FIVE

Making Contact

Fred and Wilma wanted to reach kids for Christ. They had read about teenage crime and had seen TV reports of substance abuse and suicide. They pondered what they could do to save this generation! One day, while discussing their dilemma, a thought hit Fred: why not invite friend Barney, the evangelist, to hold a youth crusade in the abandoned church next to the high school? Wilma loved the idea, and they booked Barney immediately. Soon fliers were printed and placed in strategic spots in the halls and hangouts; newspaper ads were purchased; folding chairs were rented; and banners were made. The big night came . . . but no kids did; the room was empty. For all their efforts, not a single young person attended the crusade.

We laugh at this apocryphal episode, but it is not far from reality. At first reading, we may decide that Fred, Wilma, and Barney were just naive and out of touch with kids. Instead of a crusade, they should have sponsored a concert, or a professional athlete, or free food. But the real problem lies deeper, and it is a mistake repeated by many. Simply stated, they were relying on *program* and *advertising* instead of *people* to do the ministry. The major difference between this approach and what we have called "responsible evangelism" in chapter 4 is that it depends on techniques and technology instead of relationships. Our thesis is that solid and effective ministry must be built on personal relationships, friendships, getting to know young people, and winning the right to be heard.

Before we can share the Gospel with young people and lead them to Christ, however, we have to meet them. This means going out and establishing contact, and it is hardly unique to youth work. Ask the salesman of anything from abacuses to zucchini and he will tell you that his vice president or regional manager constantly reminds him about the need for more and better contacts. There is no shortcut. If we wait for young people to come to us or to our program, we will be disappointed. Instead, we must go to them.

WHY MAKE CONTACTS?
Many years ago, an infamous thief was asked why he robbed banks. His answer: "Because that's where the money is." It may seem obvious, but the reason we must enter the world of the adolescents to reach them is because that's where they are.

Another reason we spend time "contacting" is because it works. We could spend a lot of money and design a splashy program which could attract kids, hiring their favorite rock group and providing unbelievable refreshments. But even if they came, we would have trouble getting the message across. The Gospel simply cannot be injected by hypodermic needle or absorbed by osmosis from slick media. It must be carried person to person. The most effective communication takes place when one friend tells another friend what he or she has learned or discovered. Our relationships with young people can become bridges for sharing our faith.

The most important reason we go to young people is that this is what Christ commands. Matthew 28:19 (the Great Commission) states: "Therefore go" Jesus practiced what He taught. He came to us, becoming a man and living among us (Philippians 2:5-8).

As mentioned in chapter 3, our fears often keep us from reaching out to others—fear of moving out of our comfort zones, fear of rejection. Faced with the prospect of confronting a teenager one-on-one, nothing looks quite so inviting and safe as our quiet, antiseptic offices or friendly and courteous church youth groups. But as Jesus put it, "It is not the healthy who need a doctor, but the sick" (Matthew 9:12). There are very few, if any, men and women (including professionals) who get over their fears and barriers without effort. Contacting young people is difficult for *everybody*, but there is no substitute for face-to-face involvement with individuals.

WHO CAN YOU CONTACT?

Needy young people are all around us, but often they are invisible unless we begin to look for them. Use the worksheet on page 64 to help you identify kids in your world. Take one category at a time and write down names and places. Begin with your home if you are a parent of a teenager. Think of her friends and the kids that often drop by the house. And what about his teammates or the friends who greet him as you walk together at the game or in the mall?

Next, think through your church membership. Are there Christian young people who would be willing to learn how to win their friends to Christ? Perhaps you could form a "ministry team." And there may be non-Christian kids in the sanctuary. Write down their names too.

Analyze your neighborhood. What about baby-sitters, lawn cutters, newspaper deliverers, or kids next door, across the street, or around the block? Do you live near a playground or park? Think about the young people who hang around or play ball.

There are also places where you regularly do business. Remember the teenagers who wait on you at the fast food franchise, car wash, restaurant, cleaners, etc. Who do you see on a regular basis? Or perhaps they come to where you work. List everyone you can think of.

CONTACT LIST

Place   Names

1. Home

2. Church

3. Neighborhood

4. Hangouts/Park

5. Businesses

6. Other

WHAT PROCESS CAN YOU FOLLOW?

The process of getting to know kids can be illustrated by a pyramid with three main levels—"To Be Seen," "To Be Known," and "To Be Understood." A pyramid is a good illustration because each of the higher levels builds on the lower ones. In addition, the size of each level will be smaller than the one beneath it, but it will get larger as the lower levels grow.

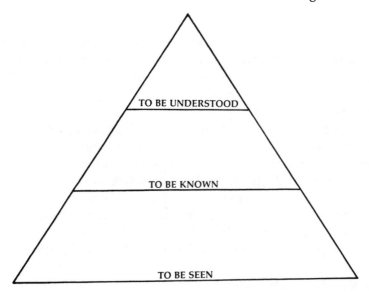

Level #1—To Be Seen

This level forms the base of the contacting pyramid. Everything you build will depend on this foundation. In some ways, the process of making contact is a numbers game. If you see 10 young people, you may get to know 4 or 5 of them and eventually have the opportunity to share the Gospel with 1 or 2. If, however, 100 kids see you, over time, 30-40 may get to know you at varying degrees of friendship. Of these, eventually about a dozen will really understand your message. This is not to say that you shouldn't become involved unless you have access to hundreds of kids. God can use you to reach the one person next door. But you will never reach more than you touch at this first level.

Being seen by kids means entering their worlds. Your very presence communicates your interest and care. Your choice, for example, to eat at the McDonald's near the high school when it is packed with students says that you are not intimidated or turned off by them or their behavior. Taking your basketball to the park and organizing a pickup game shows that you accept them as peers on the court. Going backstage after a school play or concert and congratulating the performers demonstrates your acceptance and appreciation of them as persons.

At times you will feel awkward because this is their turf, not yours. But continue these contacting efforts knowing that they form the foundation and will pay off in relationships.

Level #2—To Be Known
As you rub shoulders with young people, you will meet many of them and learn their names. And they will begin to learn about you. Remember, relationships are built as people know and understand each other. Be yourself and don't try to impress anyone. As you get to know individuals, you will have the opportunity to do things in small groups or one-on-one. This will help develop friendships. The process of building relationships will be discussed thoroughly in chapter 6.

Level #3—To Be Understood
As relationships are developed you will know young people and they will know you on a first-name basis. At this point God will give you opportunities to counsel and to share the Gospel. Because you have earned their confidence, these young people will listen to you and respect what you say. They will understand you and your message. How to relate one-to-one and how to share the Gospel will be covered in chapters 7 and 8.

HOW TO BEGIN RELATIONSHIPS
Step #1—Plan
The first step to initiating relationships with young people is to plan. Our efforts must be intentional and well thought through. This does not mean that friendships cannot be established through casual or occasional contact, but usually if we don't schedule times to meet kids, we will never get around to it.

Look at your "contact list" and choose one or two groups of youth or places where they can be found. Then check out your daily schedule and decide when you will go there. Write it down. Planning should also include thinking through who you will see and what you will say. There are two types of contacts you will make; consider both of these.

The first type are called *cold contacts*. These are kids whom

---

SOME DO'S AND DON'TS OF CONTACTING

1. *DO* remember names—whatever it takes.
2. *DO* look for ways to serve kids, do favors (e.g., tutoring, driving them home, chaperoning field trips, advising in drama, art, athletics, or some other specialty of yours).
3. *DO* remember yourself to think constantly about "walking in the Spirit." Go expectantly, asking His leadership.
4. *DO* expand your field of contacts through the kids you already know; they're usually happy to introduce you to their friends.
5. *DO* ask intelligent, feeling questions and listen, really listen, to the answers.
6. *DO* be casual, at ease, cheerful, friendly, enthusiastic.
7. *DO* develop a sense of humor, but don't try to be Johnny Carson if you're not. There are other ways to gain rapport.
8. *DON'T* try to revert to being a teenager yourself; it can't be done. Act like the adult that you are, remaining totally aware and compatible with the student scene.
9. *DON'T* talk too much about yourself.
10. *DON'T* proselytize on campus.

---

you have never met. You may have seen them before, but you don't know them and they don't know you. This is the most difficult type of contacting to do, but it can be done very effectively. As discussed previously under "To Be Seen," our purpose is to consistently enter the world of the young person, waiting for the opportunity to strike up a conversation, to break the ice.

My first walks through the high school halls as a Campus Life staff member were "cold." As I became familiar with the school, the administration, and the teachers and began to recognize certain kids from day to day, I relaxed and was able to talk to quite a few students, much sooner than I expected. Most of them were curious about who I was and why I was there, and they opened up to me as I made small talk and joked with them.

The second type of contacts are known as *warm contacts.* These are young people whom you have met before. They may be neighbors, or perhaps you've seen them at church or in the store. You may even know their names. When meeting them, you can greet them by name and discover much in common to talk about.

Jack decided to try to establish a friendship with Todd, a boy down the street who always walked his dog past the house. Knowing Todd's routine, Jack planned to leave his house for a walk at just the right time. After explaining that he had seen Todd walk by a number of times, Jack asked about the dog and then about school. They only spoke for a short while, but contact was made. The next time, Jack will be able to carry the conversation and the relationship further.

"Warm contacts" are also those whom you meet through others—your son's football teammates, your daughter's choir members. And you can ask kids to introduce you to their friends. This works well in a group. With new staff members who are fearful of walking into a teenage hangout cold, I suggest that they set up a meeting there with one of the high school students they already know. Then this person can introduce them around to the others. Warm contacting seems easier, but still it must be planned.

Step #2—Position
Planning involves scheduling the "when" of initiating relationships and the place to go. "Positioning" involves the "where," the going, the strategic placement of yourself on the scene.

Mary Ellen was concerned for the girls from the high school a couple of blocks from her house. She planned to try to meet a few of them after school, so she called and found out the dismissal time. Ten minutes before the last bell, she walked to

---

SOME CONVERSATION STARTERS

"What time does the period end?"

"When is the game this weekend?" (You've already made sure that one is scheduled.) "Are you planning to go?"

"How was your weekend?"

"How come you look so happy (depressed) today?"

"What's going on around here this week?"

"What kinds of things are you into? What's your hot interest?"

"Hi, what's your name?"

---

the main entrance so that kids would see her as they exited. After most had poured out to the busses, she walked to the group huddled against the wind who were waiting for the last bus to arrive and struck up a conversation with a few of the girls standing there. They talked about the weather, how they hated waiting for the bus, and about where they lived. Mary Ellen had positioned herself "to be seen."

On Saturdays, while cutting his grass, Wayne would notice a group of guys shooting baskets at the park near his house. A fairly good ball player a few years ago (he had even played a season on the college team), Wayne decided to see if he could join one of their games. Maybe, he thought, he could get to know some of them. The next weekend, while working on the lawn, he saw the guys begin to gather, so he stopped what he was doing, grabbed his basketball from the garage, and walked to the park. Wayne was positioning himself to be seen and to be known by this group of kids.

Another way to position yourself is to volunteer at the school. Often there is a need for chaperones for special events and trips. If you have special expertise or talent, this can be used. Certain teachers look for guest speakers who have traveled extensively or who have unique experiences or talents. And there may be opportunities to be an assistant coach or a sponsor.

In her high school and college years, Trish had been a cheerleader. Upon hearing that the high school squad had lost their sponsor, Trish volunteered to help. She was accepted and was immediately positioned to develop close relationships with many girls.

Gregg had played college football, so he volunteered to help coach the sophomore linemen; Terri had acting experience, so she began to work with the drama teacher; Mike's hobby was photography, so he took action shots at the games for the coaches and put together a slide show for their awards banquets; Grace was an excellent guitarist, so she offered to come to the music classes to demonstrate certain techniques.

Use your imagination and God-given talent to position yourself to get to know young people.

Step #3—Meet

After planning and positioning, the next step is "meeting." This simply means starting a conversation, introducing oneself, and learning names.

To begin talking to strangers requires sensitivity and tact. Of course you could always ask someone for the time or for directions, but this will only work once with an individual. A better way is to look for clues to their interests and begin there. Is he wearing a letter jacket? Talk about sports, espe-

---

FOLLOW-UP QUESTIONS

"What year are you—senior?" (Always estimate older.)
"Do you like the school? What bugs you about it? What do you like?"
"What do you do to keep yourself busy?"
"Are you working? Where? What do you do? How do you like it?"
"What are your plans after graduation?"
"Do you know a guy named _____?"

cially the sport in which he lettered. Is she carrying a load of books? Ask her which subjects she finds most difficult and which teachers she really enjoys. Other sources of clues include locations (where you meet students), their clothes, their pins, buttons, or patches, their activities (what they are doing at the time), etc. You can always ask about various current events at school.

Peggy went to the junior high gym to watch volleyball practice. Seeing a couple of girls in the bleachers, she sat next to them and began to ask about the team—their record, the best players, the coach.

To make this less frightening, practice with young people at your church. Next Sunday, walk over and strike up a conversation. Here is a "NIFTY" way to remember what to say when you meet kids:

● N-Name. Find out the person's name. Then make a mental association so that you will remember it. When you see the person again, greet him or her by name, and watch the eyes light up.

● I-Interests. Ask about activities, hobbies, and other interests. Talk about that person, not about yourself.

● F-Family. Another good conversation piece is the person's family. Where does he live? Does she have any brothers or sisters? How does he like living so close to school? And so on.

● T-Thank

● Y-You. Talk for a minute or two and move on. Don't monopolize a person's time and attention the first time you meet him or her. The idea is to build a relationship. This means seeing the person again and again. As you begin to know each other, your conversations will grow in length and depth.

Caution: Unfortunately, these days an adult's motives are often questioned. "Is he a sex pervert?" . . . "What does she want to sell?" . . . "Is he gay?" These thoughts might occur to kids and their parents. There's no way to totally avoid these questions because some people want to think the worst, but carefully avoid anything which would *cause* these questions. This means you should seek to contact kids of the *same sex* as you are. It involves being yourself, natural and relaxed. And meeting the parents (see chapter 6) will also be helpful. Of

CONTACTING AT SCHOOL EVENTS

The typical school calendar is usually crammed with events. With a bit of planning and creative thinking on your part, school events can be made into productive times to get to know students. A good suggestion would be to get a calendar of school events and together with other concerned Christian adults spend some time planning who will go to what events. Here are some guidelines and suggestions that will help you.

—Remember your objective is contacting students, not just watching the game.
—The time spent with students might be more productive and less fearful if you arrange to go with a student(s) you already know.
—Take advantage of halftimes, intermissions, before and after the event to meet students.
—Especially when you're new, fight the tendency to just sit alone in a corner, watching. Ask God to help you get up and move to get acquainted with the students. Use your imagination.
—Don't feel that you have to go to the entire game to contact profitably.
—At minor sports events such as swimming, wrestling, tennis, etc., less people usually attend, but you may have more of an opportunity to talk to kids as well as parents.

The Whole Person Survival Kit, edited by Art Deyo. (Wheaton, Ill.: Youth For Christ International, 1976).

course this will not be much of a problem with "warm contacts." If you are already well known as a neighbor, a friend's parent, a teacher, an employer, or a regular customer, they will understand that your motives are pure.

Step #4—Remember

This is the fourth and final step for the "how" stage of relationship building. It means putting faces with names and names with interests and other facts you learn about each person. Some find it helpful to buy a school yearbook and to make notes in it by the pictures. Others purchase a small notebook or keep an index card on each individual and develop a file.

Whatever your system, use something to help you remember, especially if you are meeting a lot of kids. Then use these cards, pages, or pictures as your guide for prayer and as your reminders of important facts about each individual (address, church background, school activities, year in school, family information, last conversation, spiritual interest, and others). Check the cards before you hope to see each young person again and update the cards as you aquire new information.

PRAYER—AN IMPORTANT PART

As we have discussed repeatedly, relationships are the key to ministry. Without them we become just added noise in a cluttered marketplace. The first step to establishing these relationships is "contacting"—meeting kids in their world, on their turf. Of course this entire process must be bathed in prayer. We must always be sensitive that the Holy Spirit knows us and our motives and that God cares more about these young people than we do. And He knows where they are—in fact, He may have a beautiful contact waiting for us literally around the corner. We should pray for that to happen, and we should pray about specific kids whose friendship and trust we want to develop.

KEEPING ON

With all the unstructured ambiguity of contacting, there are bound to be frustrations when kids aren't where we think they will be, act as though we don't exist, forget to meet with us, or hurry by without even a glance. But "let us not become weary in doing good, for at the proper time we will reap a harvest if we do not give up" (Galatians 6:9).

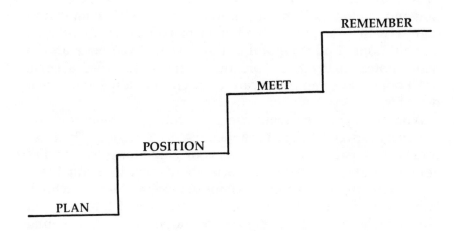

CHAPTER SIX

Winning the Right

"Who's that?" I wondered, my eyes following her every step as she walked across the hotel lobby. Her short brown hair, sparkling eyes, and musical laugh had captured my attention as I left the elevator. With hints, subtle questions, and careful listening, I soon discovered that Gail was on our Detroit Youth for Christ staff. But, unfortunately, my discovery was a bit late; our Youth for Christ convention in Toronto was almost over. Nearly a year later, I saw her again—in San Diego at the next staff conference, and I determined to make contact.

New Year's Day, in a bus heading for the Rose Parade, I overheard Gail tell a friend where she would be sitting in the Rose Bowl, and I traded tickets with another member of our group so that I could sit next to her. Our relationship began during that game as we talked about football, Campus Life, and the convention which would begin the next day. We were together again in the days to follow—sightseeing, talking, and sitting together at the final banquet.

During the next few months, our friendship grew—slowly at first through letters and occasional visits (Detroit is five hours from Chicago). Then we began to date regularly. The relationship developed, and two-and-a-half years after my initial "sighting," Gail and I were married.

In San Diego our relationship began; it has developed and grown over the past twenty-plus years, two children, and three homes. But it wouldn't have started if I hadn't made contact. Seeing Gail in Toronto was not enough. And the relationship would not have grown if we hadn't spent time together—talking, laughing, sharing experiences, and learning from each other.

Friendships take time to develop; they don't happen automatically. As we discussed in the last chapter, making contact

---

HOW DO YOU DEFINE LIFESTYLE EVANGELISM?

Joe Aldrich: I would say that it is a lifestyle that reveals the universals of God's character, like His love, holiness, compassion, and faithfulness, through the particulars of everyday living. Paul describes it as making himself a servant of everyone in order to win as many as possible for Christ. I think he's suggesting that if there's no serving, there's no winning. It's an approach to life where I use my intellectual, emotional, physical, and vocational giftedness in practical, redemptive actions that demonstrate the reality of my faith in tangible, measurable ways over a prolonged period of time. And all the while I'm looking for an opportunity to explain the worldview that stands behind my actions. But it's not just activity, it's an attitude and a lifestyle.

Life-Style Evangelism (Multnomah Press, 1981)
"Common Ground," January 1986

is the first step of personal ministry with young people. But we must build on our initial contacts to develop the relationships further. Our goal is to share the Gospel with kids effectively. We want them to listen and to believe, but first we must win the right to be heard. This can happen through "building time."

WHAT IS BUILDING TIME?
"Building time" means developing personal relationships with young people through shared activities. It is the bridge between making contact (initiating the relationship) and talking seriously and sharing the Good News. It is how students get to know more about us, find out that we're real people who live well-rounded lives and can relate to them in areas other than religion. In short, through "building time," we become known by kids.

Remember our contacting pyramid? The first level was "to be seen" and the emphasis was on becoming involved in the world of teenagers. Building relationships fits into the second level, "to be known." As we spend time with individuals and small groups of kids, they get to know us as adults who care about them.

Individuals or Small Groups
Because the purpose of building time is to develop and strengthen friendships, our attention should be focused on a few young people at a time. A large group is not very personal, and kids can be lost in the crowd. This means choosing those with whom you want to spend time. Look for kids who seem to be opening up to you or who have a special focus or need that you can fill. Or find a small group of friends or two or three kids who have the same interests.

Marty and Jeff were ardent Cub fans. After learning of their undying loyalty to the team, I suggested that we go to a game someday. They were excited about the prospect, and so we set a time and I got the tickets. While sitting in the centerfield bleachers that summer afternoon, our friendship was solidified.

Tony could play the guitar well, and he often performed at

a local coffeehouse, as well as at church banquets and other events. When Tony learned that Mario, a neighbor, was interested in the guitar, he volunteered to give him lessons. During their weekly sessions, they developed a strong friendship.

Shared Activities

Virtually endless is the list of activities which you can share with young people. The questions to ask are: "What would they like to do?" and "What need can I meet for them?" Do they like to ski? Do they need a ride to the "away" game? Would they enjoy going out for pizza?

Here are some possible building-time activities:
- sandlot football, soccer, basketball, etc.
- hiking
- picnicking
- camping
- hunting or fishing
- trips to "away" games, tournaments
- waterskiing, surfing, beach trips
- scuba diving
- shopping
- chess, Ping-Pong, tennis, racquetball, handball
- canoeing
- snow skiing, sledding, tobogganing
- eating after games
- TV or VCR watching at your house
- going to a pro game
- working out, jogging
- cooking, sewing, knitting
- playing a musical instrument
- tutoring—helping others
- making crafts

You don't have to be good at the sport or activity; you only have to be willing to try. In fact, you should choose a shared activity on the basis of the young person's most prominent interest. *Whatever he or she likes to do, you suggest doing.* If he or she is already doing it (e.g., playing football on Saturday mornings), you can coax an invitation to join. From the very beginning, you should try to discover this person's favorites

Whether you like it or not, your life is the first Bible most people ever read. That is why Jesus taught that our lives must be dominated by His love, not by religious activity alone. Our sociology must reflect our theology. How you treat people will be the clearest indication to them of who you really think God is.

Becky Pippert in *Discipling the Young Person*, Paul Fleischmann, editor (San Bernardino, Calif.: Here's Life Publishers, Inc., 1985).

by asking other kids who know him or her, by observing what the person spends a lot of time doing, or by simply asking him or her. You could suggest doing something that you know is a winner with some kids and have them round up others to make up a carload, a team, or group.

• Jennifer suggested that Sue and her friend Lori accompany her to the mall where they could walk around, shop, and grab a bite to eat.

• Alan learned of Tom's interest in drama, and so he suggested that they go to the latest production at the nearby college.

• Barb showed Jackie and Ruth how to make "radiating stars" which they could give to their moms for Christmas.

This is another area for your creativity to shine.

Getting to Know Parents

When seeking to befriend and to influence any young person, we must always remember that he or she comes from a home. Whether a young person's family situation is good or bad, broken or whole, healthy or sick, we have a responsibility to communicate with the parents. Of course you may already know them if the young person is a neighbor, or at least you may know where he or she lives. During this stage of relationship building when you will be spending time with the young person, getting to know parents is crucial. They have the right to know what is going on and who is influencing their children. Put yourself in their shoes. Wouldn't you like to know?

In addition, the most important influence on the life of any teenager has been his or her home. It has shaped him into what he is now. To understand and help him, we must relate to his home life.

This may introduce us to parents who are very rich or very poor; they may be very religious, or out of work, or alcoholic, or mentally deranged, domineering, apathetic, transient, sociable; they may even be wonderful people! But we will never know for sure until we meet them.

Usually parents will be quite anxious to meet us, especially if we have already been spending some time with their child. It is our responsibility to relieve their fear of the unknown.

So get acquainted with parents whenever you can—during a football game, after some other school event, at the store, at the post office, at church, and especially when taking a young person home. At that time you could ask, "Are your folks home? Could I stop in and meet them for just a minute?" And don't forget the phone. A quick call to ask permission, to introduce yourself, or to communicate the details of a trip will be very helpful.

Meeting parents *now* will head off a lot of problems later.

A PROCESS FOR BUILDING TIME
Step #1—Pray
As with the contacting phase, the building time must be supported and surrounded by prayer. Ask God to give you insight into your strengths and resources so that you will know what activities to plan. And ask Him to give you opportunities to suggest the right activities to the right kids. Then, as you spend time with young people, ask Him to guide what you say and do and to build the friendships.

Step #2—Plan
There will be spontaneous building times, when opportunities suddenly arise and we have to respond on the spur of the moment. We should be ready for these. For example, after a

basketball game, you may find yourself standing with three or four kids who have nothing planned. You could suggest that you all go out for pizza after which you will drive them home. Or after a pickup soccer match or backyard volleyball game, a group may decide to grab a Coke at Wendy's. You could tell them to pile into your car and you'll drive them there.

We must be ready for these sudden opportunities but must not count on them. Instead, we should *plan*.

Planning begins by taking a personal inventory to determine the skills, interests, and resources that we have which could be used effectively with young people. Everything from our hobbies to our homes are possibilities. Use the "Building Time Inventory" which follows to see what you have to offer.

Next, think about the young people you know and list their interests, needs, and what you think they might be interested in or enjoy doing. Interests could include sports, music, shopping, drama, home economics, and others. Needs would be things like "transportation to games," "practicing on the computer," "tutoring in English," and "doing a science project." Things which could spark their interest or which they might enjoy could include "going to an ethnic restaurant," "learning to water-ski," "cooking a meal for his/her girl/boy friend," "taking a trip," and others.

Of course, the better you know the person, the easier it will be to answer these questions. Use the "Youth Interests Worksheet" printed at the end of this chapter.

The next step in planning is to match the interests and needs of the specific young people with your resources. To make this stand out and to help you remember, mark the matchups on your "Youth Interests Worksheet" in red.

Now that you have a good idea of what you want to do with whom, the next step is to take your calendar and determine a good time to do it. If you know, for example, that Josh enjoys fishing and would probably be interested in going with you to the lake, find a Saturday that would be convenient for you and pencil it in. Better yet, look for a school holiday—then take a day off work and go fishing. Or if you know that Cheri and Karin are really into drama, find out when a good play is coming to town, choose a good date on your schedule,

---

BUILDING TIME INVENTORY
(Circle the resources which you have.)

Skills
    playing a musical instrument, singing, art, playing a sport, photography, tutoring, sewing, cooking, writing, speaking, acting, computer programming, carpentry, auto mechanics, other _____

_____

_____

Interests
    hobbies, connections, fishing, hunting, career, movies, plays, cars, boats, literature, music, spelunking, climbing, other _____

_____

Activities
    at school (concerts, plays, games, intramurals, shows, assemblies, classes); at church (youth group meetings, parties, special meetings, concerts, worship services); in the community (fairs, concerts, shops, festivals, restaurants, games); in the neighborhood (block parties, open houses, parties, parks, pools, recreation centers, playgrounds); other _____

_____

Equipment
    TV, VCR, car, computer, boat, 35mm camera, video camera, kitchen appliances, workshop tools, telescope, sewing machine, movies, tape recorder, stereo, tapes/records, sports equipment, other _____

_____

Facilities
    recreation room, family room, basement, garage, attic, deck, backyard, kitchen, workshop, other _____

_____

and then ask if they'd like to go. Of course the young people will have to check their schedules as well and ask their parents, but make sure yours is open before you ask (or have a few possible open dates in mind).

Note: if you are working with your own kids to reach their friends, you might consider using your home (see facilities on the "Building Time Inventory" on page 82). Have an after-game pizza party, watch a movie on your VCR (complete with popcorn), host an "open house" or a party, plan games for your son's or daughter's "sleep-over."

Step #3—Coordinate

Once your plan is in place, the next step is to ask kids to get involved. This can be as simple as suggesting that the three of you get a milkshake after the game or giving someone a ride home after school; it can be more involved like finding a time when all four of you have a Friday night and Saturday free to go camping; or it can be as complicated as arranging the itinerary, accomodations, transportation, and budget for a trip. First enlist the support of the kids and parents involved. Then finalize the details.

Step #4—Participate

This step is simply *doing* what you have planned—becoming involved in the building-time activity. As you participate, however, here are a few guidelines to keep in mind.

Be an adult. Whatever you are doing with kids, remember that you are an adult who cares about them, not an older person who has failed to grow up. I know a youth minister who was kicked out of a restaurant for giving the waitress a hard time and for being loud and obnoxious. I'm sure he thought that the kids enjoyed his antics, but, in the long run, his actions were counterproductive.

Be relaxed. Have fun and be yourself. Try to get to know the young person(s), but don't force it.

Listen and learn. Building time can be an excellent opportunity to gather a great deal of information. If you're alert enough to ask the right questions, you will learn all kinds of things about a young person's family, future plans, job, self-image,

---

DRINK THIS—YOU'RE THIRSTY!

If someone offered you a glass of water when you were not thirsty, you would say, "No, thank you."

But suppose the person is very insistent. "Listen, this is the greatest spring water in the world; I'd really like to bring you a glass of water."

"No, no thank you. I'm really not thirsty."

"Hey, listen, Jack. I really want you to drink this water."

"No, I really don't want the water."

"Drink it!"

So to end the hassle, you finally drink it down, but it is an unpleasant experience. I'm afraid this little scenario resembles a lot of our teaching in student ministries today. We say, "Take this, kid; you won't grow without it!" But there is no willingness on his part. We must spend time making people thirsty.

David Busby, in *Discipling the Young Person*, Paul Fleischmann, editor (San Bernardino, Calif.: Here's Life Publishers, Inc., 1985).

---

religious attitudes, abilities, fears, and opinions. Eventually, if you are genuine, friendly, consistent, and open, these building times will pay off in a receptive attitude toward the Gospel.

Be patient. During a building time, don't plan to discuss anything spiritual. But if something comes up in the conversation, don't squelch it. In shared activities, your role is not to be the authority figure or teacher. Instead, you are one of the group. Remember, you want to make the non-Christian young person feel totally at ease and spontaneous with you. Don't surprise him or her with your hidden spiritual agenda. Eventually God will give you the opportunity to introduce your teenage friend to your friend Jesus.

Be careful. There are some dangers to building time:

FRIENDS ARE FOR KEEPS

Friends are for keeps,
They're all we have
To get us through the day.
A smile—
A gentle word—
A special kind of love
That bonds even
The coldest hearts.
Friends are there
In your brightest moments—
And darkest destinies.
In this torn apart world
Of illusions and fantasies
Few things are certain,
Fewer uncertain;
But one thing
Forever unquestionable—
A friend;
A friend like you.

Mona Lisa Currie
11th grade student
Covington, Louisiana

• We can swerve toward what *we* like to do rather than what *kids* like to do.

• We can use building time as a copout from appointments (covered in chapter 7). If we never get around to sitting down with these same young people and telling them about Christ, we will not accomplish our goals.

• We can use building time as a replacement for contacting. If we do this, we will get to know a few individuals very well, but the base of our pyramid will shrink as we miss meeting more kids.

Continue the process. Don't think that one shared activity will build a solid friendship. Of course it depends on what you do; a weekend rappelling trip will probably accomplish more than a ride home. But relationships are built over time, and this will mean many shared events. Develop consistent contacts with certain kids and vary your experiences with them.

One year about four seniors and I would go to Howard Johnson's for ice cream every Friday after school. We established our own tradition, and during those hours we talked over just about everything. Eventually, each of those kids trusted Christ as Saviour.

And then there was Ted. During his high school years, we had scores of "building times"—everything from going to watch a professional football team practice to going with my wife and me to Florida. Years later, we remain close friends.

Step #5—Affirm
When you finish every shared activity with a teenager, let him or her know that you appreciate the time you've spent together. Affirm him as an individual; make him glad that you have been together.

Say thanks, tell him or her that you appreciate the time together, and then give that person a genuine compliment. This will take some thinking on your part so that you can tell each person something about him or her that you really appreciate. If you drive someone home after school, for example, you could say, "By the way, John, I just wanted to tell you I really enjoyed the band concert the other night. You really play a mean trumpet." If you take Christy home after the game you could compliment her on the way she dresses. After the basketball game in the park, you could tell Trent that he has a deadly jump shot.

We want kids to want to be with us because we accept them and enjoy being with them.

"Building time" is a key ingredient in personal ministry with young people. As we spend time with kids, we establish friendship, trust, respect, and communication channels. This isn't the whole ministry, but it is a necessity. Think of your close friends. They became close to you because you spent time together, laughing, talking, crying, and listening. Your shared experiences led to a solid relationship. And consider the men and women who have influenced you spiritually. Beyond their position (e.g., pastor, youth sponsor), they were people who cared and took the time to get to know you as a special individual. And you listened when they spoke. Be that kind of person to a teenager.

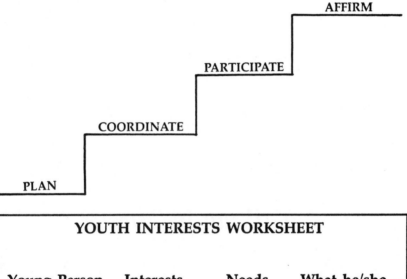

YOUTH INTERESTS WORKSHEET			
Young Person	**Interests**	**Needs**	**What he/she might enjoy**

CHAPTER SEVEN

Talking It Over

A popular high school junior, Kris often brought friends home to study, watch television, or just hang out and listen to music. Her parents, Brian and Joan, enjoyed having kids over and did their best to create a warm and accepting atmosphere. They worked at remembering names and learning each individual's activities and interests. Snacks and soft drinks were always available, supplemented at times by freshly-baked chocolate chip cookies. Sometimes Joan would throw together a unique dessert or Brian would march among the teenagers sprawled on the family room floor, carrying a huge bowl of popcorn to munch while watching the game on Saturday or Sunday afternoons. In addition to food, there were impromptu touch football games in the nearby park and intense rounds of Trivial Pursuit.

One of Kris' closest friends was Janis, a short, perky blond who stopped by often enough to be almost one of the family.

Although not a Christian, Janis had seemed open to spiritual matters and occasionally accompanied Kris to the church youth group. Kris and her parents prayed regularly for Janis and other friends, asking God to give them opportunities to share the Gospel.

One blustery November morning, Joan hurried to answer the doorbell. There stood Janis, alone with reddened eyes and shivering in the cold. Joan welcomed her in and offered a cup of hot chocolate. In the conversation which followed, Janis poured out her grief and anger. At breakfast, her parents had announced their plans for a divorce. "I knew they weren't getting along," she sobbed, "but this caught me totally by surprise. That's why I left school . . . to think and sort things out. I've been walking for a couple of hours. What am I going to do . . . and what about my little brother?"

During the next hour-and-a-half, Joan listened, dried tears, poured more hot chocolate, gave counsel, and prayed with Janis for her family. Because of their relationship, Janis came to Joan for help . . . and eventually she came to Christ.

As we build friendships with young people, counseling opportunities will arise. Kids will come to us because we are adults who have experience and knowledge and because we have demonstrated that we care about them. And the issues will range widely: strained relationships—torn families, broken romances, friendships, and cliques; emotional struggles—loneliness, guilt, depression, and joy; moral dilemmas—cheating, sex, gossip, and revenge; future issues—career, work, college, and marriage; and others. And they may even want to talk about faith, Christ, and how to know God personally.

This is the heart of the ministry, person-to-person, serious talks with young people. And it is the apex of our "contacting pyramid," "to be understood." This is when the "right to be heard" which we have been earning for so long is fully exercised.

We want and seek these one-to-one discussions, or "appointments," so that we can communicate effectively the life-changing difference that knowing Christ can make. Usually we won't reach this goal during the first appointment. The student may have a problem like Janis did or may not be

You should consider making an appointment with a student . . .
- —If you notice fairly rapid behavior change (e.g., markedly more aggressive, withdrawn, silly, sullen, superspiritual, etc.).
- —If annoying or irritating behavior continues (e.g., smart remarks, arguing, loud talking, attention-getting questions, etc.).
- —If he/she seems too quiet and withdrawn.
- —If he/she's *too* eager to be around you and to help you.
- —If you'd just like to get to know him or her better and be closer.
- —If the Holy Spirit nudges you, even if you can't think of a reason.
- —To check out rumors that he/she might be experiencing a problem (family, dating, etc.).
- —In response to a referral from another young person, a parent, a pastor, a school administrator or teacher, friend, etc.

really sure why she wants to see us and have a somewhat superficial question (e.g., "Gregg didn't speak to me all week. How can I get him back?" or "My dad's always on my case about my future. How can I get him to stop buggin' me?"), so we may not make much headway toward Jesus. But at least we can testify about the spiritual change in our own lives when the opportunity arises.

IS IT WORTH THE TIME?

Someone may ask, "With so many millions of kids to be reached, why should we take time for individual counseling? Is that the best use of our available hours? Or are we making things too complicated? Couldn't we get by with a more group-oriented format?"

The answer lies in the New Testament and our commitment

to responsible evangelism. Because we believe in "person-centeredness," there is no substitute for face-to-face discussion about Jesus Christ.

In Youth for Christ we have found that *the appointment allows us to custom-fit Christianity to a student's life and problems.* We can't go deep enough in a group meeting to hit every person's needs. Any kind of group situation calls, of necessity, for a shotgun approach; at times, however, only a rifle will do. One student may be worried about guilt, another about tensions at home, a third about sex, a fourth wants to know the basics of the Christian faith, and a fifth has intellectual objections. Each needs the personal touch.

A student "opens up" in an appointment like nowhere else. Many young people aren't really interested in knowing our Lord until they know us deeply and can do enough observing to decide whether or not our faith really works. Once this happens, they see us in an entirely new light.

Large meetings provide opportunities to communicate what *to believe; appointments allow us to* demonstrate. As we incorporate theology into a workable lifestyle, we give kids a faith with handles he can grasp. It's a little like the children's game of follow-the-leader.

Appointments allow honest feedback. Through our discussions we find out how kids are really doing and whether or not they understand the Gospel.

Appointments help spoon-fed Christians survive because we get down to real discipleship. Today's young people are open to spiritual things, yet superficial about them. Real change, as opposed to talk, is as hard-won as it always was, but the results are long-term. Personal counsel in the context of a friendship helps us spot trouble and keep the young person on track.

ME, A COUNSELOR?
Most of us will admit that we know very little about the delicate art of counseling; we have a lot to learn. Rows upon rows of library shelves are filled with books on the topic and universities offer graduate degrees in counseling.

We'll be learning how to counsel all our lives through our

THE CHARACTERISTICS
OF EFFECTIVE COUNSELORS

1. *Warmth*. This word implies caring, respecting, or possessing a sincere, nonsmothering concern for the counselee—regardless of his or her actions or attitudes.

2. *Genuineness*. The genuine counselor is "for real"—an open, sincere person who avoids phoniness or the playing of some superior role. Genuineness implies spontaneity without impulsiveness and honesty without cruel confrontation. It means that the helper is deeply himself or herself—not thinking or feeling one thing and saying something different.

3. *Empathy*. What does a counselee think? How does he or she really feel inside? What are the counselee's values, beliefs, inner conflicts and hurts? The good counselor is continually sensitive to these issues, able to understand them, and effective in communicating this understanding (by words or gesture) to the counselee.

Christian Counseling: A Comprehensive Guide, by Gary R. Collins (Waco, Texas: Word Books, 1980).

---

experiences with spouses, children, and others. We must learn from this experience but, at the same time, we must resist the urge to oversimplify counseling into a repeated pattern of pat answers (i.e., when he says this, I say that; when she does this, I tell her that). Counseling must never become mechanical; it is living, breathing interaction between two people.

But we must not let this awareness of our inadequacy paralyze us. We may not have professional training, and we will make mistakes; but we should go ahead and make the effort to counsel when we are approached by young people who trust us. Technique will improve as you learn through practice and by continually studying and searching for better ways to counsel.

PRINCIPLES OF COUNSELING

Here are a few important principles to remember when counseling a young person.

Prayerfully rely on God's wisdom and leading rather than thinking that you can solve all the person's problems. With a spirit of humility, realize that you also have unsolved problems; you are another sinful human being, just like the individual you are counseling. Don't just pray *before* the appointment; pray *during* it as well, constantly asking God what to say or not to say next.

Respond to what the person is saying and feeling, not to where you want him or her to be. Let the student begin where he feels comfortable; respond to him there. Then he will feel comfortable moving into more meaningful issues. If he senses that you know and care where he is at first, then he will trust you enough to share more difficult issues and concerns with you. Avoid stereotyping (e.g., "He's a rebel" or "She's on drugs," etc.). And don't force the person to make a spiritual commitment if she's not ready.

Accept the person just the way he or she is. This doesn't mean that you have to like everything about him or approve of everything he does. But it does mean that you allow him the freedom to be himself. He doesn't have to be the way you want him to be. Respecting him enough to allow him to be himself will do much to relieve his fear of being condemned and rejected by you.

Be as open and honest as possible with your responses to the young person. You may be the only person who loves and respects him enough to give him an accurate picture of how he comes across to others. If you are open about your own experiences and feelings, the student can gain a realistic picture of what the Christian life is. Your honesty may even prevent future disillusionment with Christianity. Also, it will show him how to be honest.

Listen intently to what the student is saying and how he or

CREATING A HELPING RELATIONSHIP

1. Can I be perceived by the other person as trustworthy, dependable, or consistent in some deep sense?
2. Can I be expressive enough as a person so that what I am will be communicated unambiguously?
3. Can I let myself experience positive attitudes toward this other person—attitudes of warmth, caring, liking, interest, respect?
4. Can I be strong enough as a person to be separate from the other?
5. Am I secure enough within myself to permit the counselee his or her separateness?
6. Can I let myself enter fully into the world of the counselee's feelings and personal meanings and see these as he or she does?
7. Can I be acceptant of each facet of this other person which he or she presents to me?
8. Can I act with sufficient sensitivity in the relationship that my behavior will not be perceived as a threat?
9. Can I free him or her from the threat of external evaluation?
10. Can I meet this other individual as a person who is in the process of becoming, or will I be bound by his or her past and by my past?

Carl R. Rogers in *On Becoming a Person* (Boston: Houghton Mifflin, 1961).

---

she is responding in the situation. Be alert and aware of what he is doing and also be sensitive to your own feelings and reactions toward him. Empathize and feel with the person rather than trying to analyze him. Pay close attention to both verbal and nonverbal behavior (e.g., voice intonation and rate, eyes watering, skin flushing, gestures, body position, etc.). Learn to trust your hunches about the person and have

THE TECHNIQUES OF COUNSELING

1. *Attending.* The counselor must try to give undivided attention to the counselee. This is done through (a) eye contact to convey concern and understanding; (b) posture, which should be relaxed rather than tense, and generally involves leaning toward the counselee; and (c) gestures that are natural
2. *Listening.* Effective listening involves hearing not only what the counselee says but what he or she is trying to say and what is left unsaid . . . and using both ears and eyes to detect messages which come from tone of voice, posture, and other nonverbal clues.
3. *Responding. Leading* is a skill by which the counselor slightly anticipates the counselee's direction of thought and responds in a way that redirects the conversation. *Reflecting* is a way of letting counselees know that we are "with them" and can understand their feelings or thinking. *Questioning,* if done skillfully, can bring forth a great deal of useful information. The best questions are those which require at least a sentence or two from the counselee. *Confronting* means presenting some idea to the counselee that he or she might not see otherwise. *Informing* involves giving facts to people in need of information. *Interpretation* involves explaining to the counselee what his or her behavior or other events mean. *Supporting and encouraging* are important parts of any counseling situation, especially at the beginning.
4. *Teaching.* All of these techniques are really specialized forms of psychological education. The counselor is an educator, teaching by instruction, by example, and by guiding the counselee as he or she learns to cope with the problems of life.

Christian Counseling: A Comprehensive Guide, by Gary R. Collins (Waco, Texas: Word Books, 1980).

the courage to check those hunches out. Ask if your perception is correct. One of the most important processes in effective communication is listening carefully.

Be a human being; have the courage to be imperfect. All you have in any counseling relationship is yourself. Your skills and techniques are only as good as you are effective in building healthy relationships. Young people are much more willing to talk meaningfully with a warm-blooded person with whom they can identify than they are with a lofty image of perfection and saintliness. Be open to give and receive both positive and negative feedback.

Try to help the student learn how to solve his or her problems and make his or her own decisions. Teach her that she can depend on her own God-given brains and character. Don't feed your own ego by fostering her dependency on you. You are not an answer machine or a dispenser of pre-packaged frozen problem-solving formulas. Help her to become independently dependent on Jesus Christ.

Integrate prayer into your counseling in a way that shows the young person that God is concerned and can help. But do not use prayer as an easy answer or as an excuse for not working with the person at a deeper level where he is really hurting.

It is very important to remember that *all behavior is purposeful.* Do not discount seemingly silly and pointless behavior as unimportant. Try to help the young person understand the goals (e.g., acceptance from others, feelings of power or importance, revenge, attention, self-concealment, etc.) for which she is striving. Help her evaluate her goals and then encourage her to develop more constructive behaviors and habit patterns for achieving her goals.

Be aware of your abilities and capacities as a counselor. Don't be afraid to stretch yourself by working in difficult counseling situations. Remember, however, that you are working with valuable human beings. When you think you are beyond the limits of your present abilities, don't hesitate to refer the individual to someone you think is more qualified (e.g., pastor, school counselor, psychologist, social worker, psychiatrist, medical doctor, etc.). Tell the person why you

---

THE ADOLESCENT'S DEVELOPMENTAL TASKS

As you think of the teenagers that you know and perhaps work with, consider their actions in light of the developmental tasks which are theirs to accomplish. There are essentially three psychological tasks that today's teenagers need to accomplish:

1. To develop a sense of personal identity that consistently establishes who he or she is as an integrated individual throughout each life role, separate and different from every other person.

2. To begin the process of establishing relationships that are characterized by commitment and intimacy.

3. To begin making decisions leading toward training and entry into a particular occupation.

Dr. G. Keith Olson, in *Counseling Teenagers* (Loveland, Colo.: Group Books, 1984)

---

are making the referral and help him make the transition any way you can.

THE INITIAL CONTACT
Appointments are initiated either by the young person or by you.

The Young Person's Initiative
Janis contacted Joan because her need was great and because she knew that Joan would be understanding, loving, and helpful. If we have developed friendships with kids and if they know that we will be ready and willing to help, they may ask for advice and counsel, especially when faced with a difficult or painful problem. When this happens, we should be

ready to listen carefully, take seriously their concerns, offer insight, and suggest a plan of action.

Most kids, however, will not seek us out. Even if they respect and like us a great deal, they won't want to bother us with their problems, assuming that we are too busy or that we would be disappointed with them. We can overcome this barrier, however, by dropping hints about our concern and availability.

Every Campus Life meeting closes with this kind of statement: "If you want to get together and talk . . . about anything . . . just let me know. That's why I'm here—to listen and to be a friend. So if I can help in any way or if you just want to talk to someone, or maybe you want to know more about what we discussed in the meeting tonight, just check that box on the card. I'll see you or call you, and we'll set up a time to get a Coke and talk the whole thing over." By doing this, the staff member broadcasts the fact that when needed, he or she will be there.

Dropping hints during casual conversation is more difficult, but with a little imagination, it can be done. You could introduce a serious but unthreatening topic and go from there, for example: "What do you plan to do after high school?" (pause for answer) "I know it was a pretty confusing time for me, trying to sort it all out. We'll have to get together some time and talk about it. Maybe you can learn from my mistakes."

Or you could talk in general about a felt need, for example: "One of the most difficult things to figure out is dating. I think it should be outlawed as 'cruel and unusual punishment'! I guess I'm on a personal crusade for getting to know girls (or guys) without all that pressure."

Another possibility would be to let the person know of your interest in his or her particular situation (e.g., "How's everything on the home front?"), your expertise (e.g., "I used to be a school counselor, so I know what many kids are going through"), or your experience (e.g., "I've had the chance to talk to some kids about . . . ").

Your Initiative
As implied above, most of the time, we will have to make the

TO COUNSEL OR TO CONVERT?

A primary emphasis in Christian work is proclaiming the "Good News" of Jesus Christ. Some Christians fear that evangelism will lose out if church workers accept a style of helping that is not directly preaching or witnessing. When preaching or teaching methods are not sufficient to bring a person to Christ or help him solve problems, counseling strategies are very useful. Counseling is compatible with converting activities when a person's needs are used to determine what styles of help are correct.

The Youth Leader's Source Book, edited by Gary Dausey, Grand Rapids: Zondervan, 1983.

---

first move . . . take the initiative. This will not be difficult, especially if the relationship is strong. It just means to come out and suggest getting together. Here are some possibilities.

"Hey, let's get together for a Coke."

"We should probably get together and talk things over some time. How about tomorrow after school?"

"I heard that things are getting pretty tough at your house. Do you want to get together and talk about it?"

"You mentioned at the game that you've been thinking seriously about life lately. Let's set up a time when we can talk that through a little deeper. I've got some ideas that I think might help."

Walking through the halls just after school, I spotted Betsy walking toward me. A regular attender at Campus Life, she had listened carefully to the wrap-ups at the end of the meetings. As the lead in the school musical, the night before was their last performance. She approached, and I said, "Hi." I complimented her on the performance, adding, "I've been in musicals and plays too. They're great! The only trouble is that when they're over, you feel empty inside, like something's missing." She agreed and began to share how she felt. Continuing our talk on the school steps, I was able to bridge into a discussion of the Gospel, and eventually she prayed to receive Christ as her Saviour. God gave me the opportunity, and obviously the Holy Spirit was working in both of us to bring us together. My hints led to a one-on-one conversation which led to Christ.

Another way to initiate conversation is through an outside resource. After seeing a thought-provoking television show or movie, you could discuss its meaning and implications. Or you could invite a friend to hear an outstanding Christian entertainer or speaker. Afterwards you could ask, "What did you think about what _____ said tonight?" and then follow up on the answer.

Books, magazines, and pamphlets also make excellent discussion starters. After a Campus Life meeting, Terry approached me and said, "I want to talk to you about what you said tonight, but I don't even know what to ask." I gave him a book and suggested we discuss it after he read it. We did and had a terrific series of appointments. Eventually Terry committed his life to Christ. *Campus Life* magazine can be a good discussion-starter. Each issue has real-life stories, fiction, and regular columns which cover the gamut of adolescent concerns and needs. You could either subscribe for your teenage friend or give her a copy to read, recommending an article or two that you know she would enjoy. Later, ask what she thought about a specific story or column.

If the student turns you down and simply doesn't want to talk, respect his or her wishes. He will probably change his mind before long if you continue to show concern and availability. Most young people, however, will say yes. Be open and honest about why you want to get together, never leaving the person wondering whether you think he has some terrible problem that you're going to straighten out. He will be much more open and receptive in the appointment if you don't try to trick him into seeing you.

THE PROCESS

As with initiating relationships (contacting) and with building relationships (building time), there are four simple steps to remember concerning personal talks with individuals (appointments). These are *plan, schedule, help,* and *close.*

Step #1—Plan

Planning simply means that appointments should be part of your ministry strategy. I cannot stress this enough. Consider again our contacting pyramid. It is important to have a large base of contacts, "to be seen." And we must build on those contacts by spending time with individuals and small groups, establishing friendships, "to be known." But our ultimate goal is to communicate with individuals the life-changing message of Jesus Christ. This is the apex of the pyramid, "to be understood." Using another picture, if we have built the relationship bridge, we must be willing and ready to cross it.

Under "remember" in chapter 5, I suggested tracking your relationships with kids on index cards or another device. These cards will help you pray specifically for individuals, and they will help you see where the relationships are going. You should continually pray for opportunities and think about the right time to approach each person with the plan of salvation.

As stated above, they may come to us asking for counsel and advice; but more often, we will have to take the initiative.

Step #2—Schedule

This means carving out time in your calendar to get together with individuals. After the student has agreed to talk things over, take out your schedule and set a time that is best for both of you. When doing this, consider two things: place and time.

Arrange to meet a young person (or even pick him up if you're afraid he may not show) somewhere that is convenient to both of you but preferably on his turf: a coffee shop near school for a meal or a snack (let him know whether or not you're buying); the school parking lot; maybe your home; even somewhere outdoors, weather permitting. Let the student recommend a place, just so it's at least semiprivate. If you think he could get emotional, lean toward a more private site. Your car or his is fine, as long as you and the counselee are of the same sex.

If, in the course of setting up the appointment, you sense

that the guy or girl would like to back out of it, don't pressure him or her. Just let him know that you are available anytime he decides that he wants to talk to you.

If the student seems forgetful, don't hesitate to call the night before with a reminder about the appointment. Doctors and dentists do that even with adults.

There are six basic time slots for personal talks, and it makes a difference what kind of an appointment you schedule at each time.

Early morning tends to be a more superficial time; the young person's brain (and perhaps yours) probably isn't out of low gear yet. And, depending on when school begins, this can be very early. You will find it more difficult to get down to business. Thus, early morning is better for warming up to an individual and getting to feel at ease with each other. Save the really heavy conversation for next time. You also may have to provide transportation.

Lunch is a good time when there is an open campus, where kids like to get away to the nearest fast food chain. You won't be able to cover a bulk of material during lunch, however, because you'll be occupied with driving somewhere, eating, and driving back. Like several other slots in the day, you will have a deadline—which isn't necessarily bad. It can help you make good use of your limited time together.

During the day is another appointment possibility on open campuses, provided the administration doesn't mind and you can make time in your schedule. A fifty-minute period is about the right length, and kids like something different to do during their free period. This time slot involves neither food nor driving. Be careful, however, about talking about spiritual matters on campus.

After school is just about perfect; the young person's mind is relaxed, and there's no deadline. You may not even have to provide transportation if he or she can catch a late bus. Another possibility is during workouts and practices that you normally attend anyway, assuming the coach or sponsor doesn't mind.

After a group meeting can work well, especially if the speaker has communicated effectively and you are driving the student home. You could go to a restaurant for dessert and conversation.

Weekends allow the greatest flexibility, especially if your job or their homework and extracurricular activities make it difficult for you to find time during the week. Appointments can happen beneath the stands right during football games. Specially scheduled appointments (Saturday morning, Sunday afternoon, etc.) may take longer simply because you have no deadline and will tend to talk about a variety of topics. You may want to plan to do something together so that the appointment is really building time with a purpose.

Step #3—Help

This is the meat of the appointment, where you get serious and discuss things in depth. In a counseling situation, your goal should be to *help* the person through his or her problem by listening and offering suggestions for corrective action. In a witnessing situation, your goal should be to *help* by confronting the person with his or her need for Christ and how to become a Christian.

The counselor who is a follower of Jesus Christ has the ultimate, overarching goal of showing people how to have an abundant life and of pointing individuals to the eternal life which is promised to believers. Notice the words "ultimate" and "overarching" in the previous sentence. If we take the Great Commission seriously, we will have a strong desire to see all of our counselees become disciples of Jesus Christ. If we take the words of Jesus seriously, we are likely to reach the conclusion that a fully abundant life only comes to those who seek to live in accordance with His teachings.

Christian Counseling: A Comprehensive Guide, by Gary R. Collins (Waco, Texas: Word Books, 1980).

Before you go for the appointment, spend whatever time it takes to get ready. Research the person's background and interests; check your record to see what you have said to him previously. Spend time in prayer, admitting to God that you may not be His best representative in this situation but that you want to do your best and need all the help He can give.

En route, focus your thoughts entirely on the young person and review everything you know about him or her. By the time you pick him up, you should be totally involved in his world and problems.

Be on time—if you're not, the student won't wait long before she leaves, reminding herself never to ask for another appointment with you. If she's late, wait for her; even go looking for her if you have a clue to her whereabouts and think she may have forgotten.

When you finally do get together, be as casual as possible. Talk about the young person's interests, and just have a good time together. But don't spend too much time with small talk if *the student* has initiated the appointment. I've had kids interrupt my banter about football or school to say, "What I really want to talk about is. . . . "

Shift the conversation, starting off with the assurance that whatever the young person says is confidential unless it will cause him or others harm. Reassure the student that you've talked with others about all kinds of things, so he or she probably won't shock you. Thank the student again for wanting to share with you, and then say something like: "I'll just listen now, and you tell me what you've been thinking about."

What the young person says *may or may not be the real problem.* Often he will start off with a surface issue, just to get your reaction before moving on to what is really bothering him. So be alert. Your time is valuable, and you may have to steer the conversation back on track more than once.

You probably will not be able to solve everything in a single appointment, so leave it open to get together again. It is important, however, to make sure that you understand where the person stands in his problem or in relation to Christ so that you will know what course of action to suggest. Be sure to clarify often (e.g., "Do you mean . . . ?" "I hear you saying that . . . ", etc.). Then give practical steps that the person can take—concrete counsel which can help him or her toward a solution.

If, for example, a young person is having a conflict with a parent, you could have her outline two or three actions she can take which will alleviate tension or build a better relationship (e.g., "Clean your room *before* your mom asks," "Do your chores without complaining and then ask, 'Is there anything else you want me to do?' " "Count to ten silently before talking back with a bad attitude or in anger," etc.).

If the young person is close to making a commitment to Christ, but is not quite ready, you could give him or her a New Testament and suggest reading a specific chapter or two. You might also provide a copy of a Gospel presentation (such as "Your Most Important Relationship" mentioned in chapter 8) and have the student read it through and look up the verses. Or suggest another reading assignment.

It is important to give the individual a specific action plan which will help with the immediate need and lead to the next step.

Step #4—Close
This is where your appointment ends. It is important that you and the young person understand that your time together has been valuable, that you have covered important facts and feelings, and that you agree on the next step. As you close, therefore, *thank* the person for sharing with honesty, vulnerability, and openness. Be sure to communicate that you really appreciate this person and enjoy the friendship.

Next, *review* what you have covered together, the problem, the counsel, and the assignment (plan of action).

Finally, *set a time* for the next time you will get together when you will follow up on the assignment and continue the discussion. If it is appropriate, you can offer to close in prayer, for the person, the situation, and the next steps the young person will take.

Specific closings for Gospel presentations will be discussed in the next chapter.

Getting to the place where we can have personal counseling appointments with young people should be the heart of our ministry. We should make sure that all we do points toward this goal . . . and then we should be prepared to listen to the young person, offer helpful counsel, and present the Good News of Christ when we can.

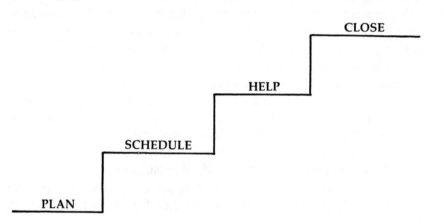

CHAPTER EIGHT

Crossing the Bridge

Once upon a time, there was a bright knight, resplendent in silver-plated armor. He was a knight to remember, for beneath his metal suit beat a soft heart; he was a man of compassion. On the way to countless battles or dragon-slaying adventures for the king, often he would detour to assist helpless folk or rescue a distressed maiden or two.

One lazy afternoon, breathless and urgent word burst upon him as he sat in the palace courtyard, carefully shining his coat. "Yonder, in Lost Trailia lieth a people terrorized and enslaved by the great giant Gression!" gasped the messenger. "They have no hope save for thou, my lord," he concluded in perfect old English.

Fully aware of his pledged and sacred duty, the knight quickly donned his armor and strode to his steed. Riding rapidly to the rescue, however, he began to analyze and assess the situation. You see, Lost Trailia lay just beyond his kingdom, separated by a vast gulf and bordered by jagged cliffs. If he would rescue with success, he must determine how to cross that canyon. This would be no easy task.

But then like a shaft of brilliant sunlight breaking through storm-laden clouds, the answer came to him. He would build a bridge! And he knew how, having learned elementary bridge construction in knight school.

Arriving at cliff's edge, the knight quickly dismounted and removed his armor. Then he began to gather the necessary bridge-building materials. In just a few days, he had strung rope across the ravine on which he could maneuver, but only very cautiously.

"This is good," he thought, "but I can do better. In fact, the bridge should be sturdier and safer, especially if it must support my horse." And so he continued to work, adding ropes and wooden planks.

"This is very good," he mused, "but perhaps it should be stronger. It is fine for such a knight as this, but what of future travelers?" And so he set to work again, improving the strength of his bridge, all the while gaining valuable experience and expertise as a bridge-builder. Onlookers proffered compliments on his progress and gave their suggestions for improving the stability and enhancing the aesthetics of the structure. "Thank you," he would reply modestly, "but it is all in a knight's work."

Soon the knight's reputation as a master bridge-builder spread far and wide, and often he would break from his work to consult with others along the gulf. He was even honored as the "bridge-builder of the year" by the king who loved his labors because of the tourist revenue brought to the kingdom.

"I've never felt so fulfilled," thought the knight. "Surely this is my calling . . . my destiny." And he spent his days building bridges which he called "Knight Crossings."

"But," you may ask, "what ever became of the Lost Trailians?"

They continued to be terrorized and enslaved by brutal Gression—but you will have to admit that they certainly had a beautiful bridge to the kingdom.

This little fable illustrates the tension that exists between building bridges and crossing them. To be responsible and effective in reaching lost young people, we must build relationship bridges so that we can bring them the Gospel. But we must also *cross those bridges*. Like the knight, it would be easy to become proficient at bridge-building, contacting scores of kids, establishing friendships with many, and even having heart-to-heart talks with a few. But unless we tell them the Good News, we will have failed. We must be ready, willing, and able to confront them with the necessity for personal commitment to Christ.

BUILD ON THE RELATIONSHIP
The process of "crossing the bridge" begins when we first recognize that the bridge between young people and the Gospel exists and that it can hold our weight.

Bridge-building Tool #1—Don't fear rejection.
If you have a good relationship with a young person, you can be open with him or her, and you can discuss just about anything. Think about your closest friend other than your spouse. How would you feel if he or she told you about an important discovery, a critical decision, or a pressing problem? You would listen carefully and offer congratulations, help, or advice. Certainly you would not be offended because she was honest and vulnerable.

It's the same with our young friends. Some youth workers are afraid that they will turn kids off if they mention "God," "Jesus," or "religion," and so they hesitate or even refuse to risk sharing the Gospel. But those fears are unfounded and even tragic. Obviously we should be careful with our communication methods, but we must not let this fear immobilize us.

Bridge-building Tool #2—Be yourself.
When I was a teenager, Tom, a former member of our church youth group, returned from Bible college during Christmas vacation. Good-natured and easygoing, Tom was well-liked. We welcomed him and peppered him with questions about his post-high-school experiences. And we thought it was great that he was studying for the ministry. Later in the meeting,

There was a young man who was very much in love with his girlfriend, and he decided that he wanted to marry her. He wasn't sure how to go about it, though, so he sought advice from his uncle. "Uncle," the boy said, "I have a real problem. I am so much in love with my girlfriend, and I really want to ask her to marry me. I really don't know what to say. How do I propose and what should I say?"

The uncle answered, "Son, if you love that girl, there ain't no wrong way."

If you have a heart that's motivated by love for God and the desire to share the Gospel, and you love the person, there is really no wrong way to tell him or her about Jesus.

Don Mardock, Youth for Christ Regional Field Director

our youth leader asked Tom to close in prayer. I couldn't believe what I heard. Fun-loving, one-of-the-boys Tom lowered his voice to a deeper pitch and spoke with a quiver in King James, "thees," "thous," and "shouldests." He had shifted into a "spiritual" personality for his prayer.

We must be careful not to do this when sharing the Gospel with young people. For whatever reason, it is a common habit to change voice level and intonation when speaking of spiritual matters. Instead, we should talk naturally, telling our friend about something that is very important to us. As Ron Hutchcraft says, "Witnessing is introducing my friend on earth to my friend in heaven."

So when you tell a young person about Christ, be yourself.

Bridge-building Tool #3—Use language they understand.
When shopping for a computer, I was easily intimidated by sales people who tried to explain the features and advantages of their products. Using foreign terms and clichés, it was as though they were speaking another language. Although they were trying to *sell* me something I was interested in, they

PRINCIPLES FOR SHARING CHRIST

1. *Find out where the hurt is so you can apply the medicine.* People come to Christ because they see that they *need* Him. Just as they only want aspirins when they have headaches, they only want the benefits of the death of Christ when they are aware of personal needs. Otherwise, when someone says, "Christ died for you," they are likely to reply, "So what?"

2. *De-church your vocabulary.* Foreign missionaries sometimes spend a year or even longer in language study. High school students will generally not hear what we intend for them to hear when we use words like "believe" (he believes in gravity, George Washington, music, God, pizza . . .), "saved" and "repent" (bad sawdust-trail connotations), "sin" (that's a word thought to be reserved for murder, adultery, etc.), "accept/receive Christ" (Catholics "receive Christ" every Sunday in the mass; others find the phrase abstract) or "become a Christian" (which definition?).

3. *Make sure he or she understands the disease of sin which rages inside him.* We have sinned. We are rebels. We must surrender and stop this guerilla war against God. Repentance means actually to change one's mind-set about sinning, and any worthwhile decision for Christ must include repentance (even though we may not use the word) as well as faith.

4. *Maintain the attitude of a happy beggar!* D.T. Niles of Ceylon once put it, "Evangelism is simply one beggar telling another beggar where to find food." The appointment is not an indoctrination session; it is a time for sharing the amazing relief you've found with someone else who needs it just as badly.

couldn't speak in terms I could understand.

Whatever the field of reference, it is easy to lapse into jargon or clichés understood only by insiders. And this is true with Christianity. But if we want young people to understand the message and to respond to Christ, we must use words and expressions which they understand, and which meet some of the following criteria:

● *Nonthreatening.* To most people, "non-Christian" is synonymous with "heathen" or "un-American." No one likes being a "non" anything. When you talk with people about Christ, therefore, be careful not to erect these emotional or intellectual communication barriers.

● *Free from clichés.* Words like "saved" and "born-again" are easily misunderstood by those outside the faith. Even words like "sin" and "heaven" must be carefully explained. I remember telling a young person that he must *"accept* Christ as his personal Saviour."* Later I learned that he heard me say *"except* Christ. . . ."* As you share, think about what the person must be hearing and thinking. Ask if he understands or has any questions before proceeding further.

● *Geared to the individual.* Each person to whom we speak is a complex human being with special needs and concerns and a unique personal history; therefore, we must not use a canned sales-pitch approach. Instead, we should tailor each Gospel presentation to the individual.

Bridge-building Tool #4—Don't forget to pray.
As has been mentioned before, prayer is the key to all we do. Each step of the bridge-building process must be immersed in prayer. Pray before meeting with the young person. Then as you talk, continue to breathe your petitions heavenward. Ask God for sensitivity for the young person and for His leading, for the right words to say, for His timing, and for the courage to speak. And pray for the young person, that he or she would be open to the Gospel.

HOW TO USE OPENERS
To "cross the bridge" we must take the first step. Here are some ways to begin the conversation and to focus the atten-

tion on Christ.

Discussion Starters

We examined a few of these in chapter 7. "Discussion start-ers" are questions or statements which give the person per-mission to talk openly about his or her thoughts, feelings, and ideas as they relate to the Gospel.

These are not gimmicks to be thrown into any conversation, but we should be ready to use lines like these when the op-portunities arise. You could say:

• "What did you think about the way that film pictured peo-ple who believe in God?"

• "With so many churches, hospitals, and organizations dedi-cated to the memory of Jesus Christ, He must have been a remarkable person. What do you think about Him?"

• "Have you given much thought to life after death? What do you think happens after we die?"

• "The Bible is the world's number-one bestseller. What do you remember from what you've read in the Bible?"

WHAT HAVE YOU FOUND TO BE MOST EFFECTIVE IN BRINGING PEOPLE TO FAITH IN CHRIST?

Joe Aldrich: I am increasingly finding literature to be very effective. I give away a lot of books in our neighborhood. For instance, one of our neighbors who died recently was a radiant Christian and well-loved in the neighborhood. One teenaged boy was particularly close to her. I gave him Don Baker's little booklet on "Heaven" and wrote a note in the front of it that said, "This is where our friend Frankie is now, and I thought you might like to read this."

From *Life-Style Evangelism* (Multnomah Press, 1981). "Common Ground," February 1986

● "You go to church? Why?"
● "Where are you in your progress toward God?"

Discussion Guides

Here are some possible ways to begin the conversation and to steer it toward a Gospel presentation.

● *Definition*. Ask, "How would you define a *true* Christian?" The young person will probably respond that a true Christian is someone who really believes in Christ and who does what He says. (If he or she has no idea or a strange concept, you can gently lead them back to the person of Christ—e.g., "How does Christ fit into your definition?")

In any case, after the person responds to your statement, ask: "Would you say that you are a true Christian by that definition, or that you are in the process?"

If the person is not a believer, he probably will say that he is "in the process." Then you can say, "Let me take a few moments to show you how you can know for sure where you stand with God—how you can become a true Christian."

● *Heaven*. This discussion guide uses very simple questions to underscore a profound truth. Begin by asking: "Do you think heaven is perfect?"

If the person thinks about what you have asked and is honest, he or she will say something like: "Yes, of course . . . if it weren't perfect, it wouldn't be heaven."

Then you can ask, "Are you perfect?"—to which the person is likely to answer, "No, of course not—far from it."

After this you should say, "Then how do you expect to fit in?"

The truth is that something has to happen to us to make us ready for heaven, for the presence of our holy God. It is not enough to be a great person, for even if we had only sinned *once*, we would be unfit for heaven.

● *Church*. If the young person has some kind of church background you could ask, "What did you learn about God in your years in church?"

After the young person shares his or her ideas, you can begin to talk about what God is really like.

The point here is that many young people don't believe in

God or they think very little about Him because they have a misconception of what He is like. Picturing God as an old man with a long flowing beard and white hair who sits at the edge of the universe, they assume that He is out of touch and really doesn't care about what they are going through. In reality, God knows them perfectly, loves them completely, and wants the very best for their lives. And this all-powerful, loving Creator sent Jesus to die for them. He stands ready to change them from the inside out.

• *Decision.* A very helpful question is: "In your sixteen years, what have you decided about Jesus Christ?"

In a subtle way, this question forces the teenager to think through his or her ideas about Christ. After he answers, you can open God's Word together and see what Jesus was really like and what He taught.

• *Doorkeeper.* A version of this question has been used very effectively by the "Evangelism Explosion" program of Coral Ridge Presbyterian Church in Ft. Lauderdale, Florida. Ask: "If you were standing at the door to heaven, and the doorkeeper said, 'Why should I let you in?' what would you say?"

The answer to this question will give you the opportunity to explain that it is only by *faith* that a person is made right with God and can have eternal life.

Illustrations

Sometimes it will be necessary to use illustrations to help young people pinpoint where they stand in their relationship with God. I have found the following ones to be very useful.

• *Faith continuum.* Explain that becoming a Christian involves faith. But faith is more than just believing that certain things are true. It has three parts, all of which are important. Draw an arrow on a piece of paper, from left to right, as you give each part to illustrate that each one builds on the other.

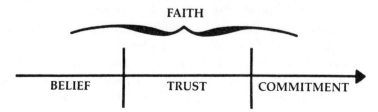

Then explain that first of all there is belief in the facts. This is an important first step, and it means believing that certain things are true. To become a Christian, a person must believe that God exists; that Jesus, God's Son, came to earth, lived a sinless life, died on the cross for our sins, and rose again; and that only through Christ can anyone experience God's forgiveness and eternal life. But just believing these *facts* is not enough.

The second part of faith is *trust* in the person. This means believing that God wants the very best for us and that He will do what He says. It goes beyond the facts of the life, death, and resurrection of Christ to knowing that God will keep His promises. He will give us eternal life if we truly believe in Him. But even having belief and trust is not enough.

The final part of faith is commitment of one's life. This means giving our lives to Christ, without reservations, to do with as He pleases. It means saying to Him, "Come in and take over . . . I'm yours."

This is the total "faith package"—belief, trust, and commitment.

After you work through the above explanation, have the young person look again at the arrow and ask, "Where would you place yourself on this line?"

Where the person places himself will determine your next step. You may have to talk about the facts . . . or about God's love . . . or about having courage to take that final step. In addition, you and the young person will understand where he or she stands in the journey of faith.

● *Marriage parallel.* This illustration compares a person's relationship with God to the progression in the relationship between a man and a woman. Again, as you explain this, write the key words on a line, moving from left to right.

When using this illustration, I talk about Gail and me saying something like: "There was a time in our relationship when we were strangers." (Write "strangers" on the line.) "That is, we didn't even know that the other person existed. Eventually, however, we saw each other and were introduced; we became acquaintances." (Write "acquaintances" on the line.) "At this point, we knew each other, but we didn't know much more than each other's names.

"As we began to get to know each other, we became friends." (Write "friends" on the line.) "We felt comfortable in each other's presence and could discuss a variety of topics.

"Eventually our friendship progressed to where we started dating." (Write "dates" on the line.) "We really enjoyed each other's company and were in the 'like/love' stage.

"As 'like' turned into 'love,' we moved into the engagement stage." (Write "fiancés" on the line.) "This meant that we had determined that we wanted to spend the rest of our lives together; we were planning to make a lifetime commitment to each other.

"Finally, we were married." (Put a big "X" on the line.) "We made that commitment. This ended a long process in the development of our relationship, but it also began a new life of living together in love."

After giving this illustration, say something like: "Our relationship with God is very similar. There are those who are 'strangers' with God. In other words, they might say, 'God who?'

"Other people would consider themselves 'acquaintances' with Him. They know a little about Him.

"Some people would say that they are 'friends' with God. They occasionally visit His house and talk things over. Of course this friendship level can even be deeper, as with 'very good friends.'

"Others, of course, would say they were 'dates.' This means that they are taking a serious look at their relationship with God.

"And some would say that they are 'engaged'; that is, they have decided to make a lifetime commitment to Him but haven't yet taken that step.

"And, of course, there are those who have given their lives to Christ and are now living with Him in a very close relationship."

After explaining the parallel ask: "Thinking of your relationship to God this way, at what stage would you place yourself?"

After the young person answers, you can explain how he

or she can move to the next stage in a relationship with God.

TURN THE CORNER

Whether counseling a young person about a specific problem or using one of the discussion starters, discussion guides, or illustrations explained above, eventually you must give the specifics of the Gospel.

Counseling

After giving counsel and helpful advice, if you think the person would be open (and you feel the "nudge" of the Holy Spirit), turn the conversation directly toward Christ in one of the following ways.

● *Power.* Say, "I want to encourage you to do what we have talked about . . . but before we go, I have to be completely

---

QUESTIONS

This method of sharing the Gospel does not make a formal presentation; instead, the student's existing knowledge is pulled out by answering the following questions until he virtually spells out salvation for himself. If he does not know the right answer at any point, insert it from Scripture.

1. Who is Jesus Christ? (The Son of God)
2. Why did He come to this world? (To die)
3. Why did He die? (For sin)
4. Whose sin did He die for? (Everyone's)
5. Does that mean His death automatically covers everyone? (No)
6. Then how do you cash in on it?

At this point, the student may be stumped. Proceed with the final point of an evangelism presentation.

---

honest. Making any of these changes will be difficult if not impossible on your own. You need the *power* to change. This power comes from God who wants to work in and through you. Here's what happened to me. . . ." At this point, give your personal story of how you came to faith in Christ. Philippians 2:12-13 would be helpful here as well.

• *Religion.* Say, "We've been talking about _____ for quite a while now, and I think we've made some progress. But let me ask you this: How does your religion, faith, or Christianity relate to this area of your life?" (Or you could say, "How does your faith work in your life?") After the person gives an answer, you can explain the difference that knowing Christ makes in yours.

Direct Presentation

Direct presentation occurs when you have moved from another subject into a discussion of the Gospel or when discussing Christ is the reason for your appointment.

There are many helpful tools on the market which will help you explain how to become a Christian. Whatever you use, be sure to understand and know it fully so that you aren't a slave to a piece of paper or particular wording (like a sales presentation). Youth for Christ/USA has an excellent booklet entitled "Your Most Important Relationship" (available through YFC Sales, phone: 312-668-6600). Most Christian bookstores offer a variety of booklets and tracts which summarize the Gospel.

Whatever tool you use, start by going through the major points, outlining each one on a piece of paper or napkin (whatever you find handy). Then give the person the booklet to read later. Or, read and discuss the booklet together. In either case, preface your presentation by saying something like: "Here's something that I found helpful. It explains how a person can begin a friendship with God."

What follows are the main points and supporting Bible verses for "Your Most Important Relationship." A sample of the booklet is included at the end of this chapter.

You were created with value and worth. God wants your life to count. Did you know . . .

1. God loves you and created you to have a personal relationship with Him.

- God created you. *Psalm 139:13-14*
- God loves you. *John 3:16*
- God wants you to know Him. *John 17:3*

2. Our sin keeps us from having a personal relationship with God.

- What is sin? *James 4:17*
- Who has sinned? *Romans 3:23*
- What happens when we sin? *Isaiah 59:2; Romans 6:23*

3. Only through Jesus Christ can you have a personal relationship with God.

- Why Jesus Christ? *John 14:6*
- Why did Jesus Christ have to die? *1 Peter 3:18*
- Why did Christ rise from the dead? *1 Corinthians 15:3-6*

4. You must personally respond by trusting Jesus Christ as Saviour and Lord.

- You respond with trust in Christ. *Ephesians 2:8-9*
- You respond by turning to God from sin. *Acts 3:19*
- You respond by receiving Christ. *John 1:12*

5. Your trust in Jesus Christ begins a lifelong relationship.

- God commits Himself to you. *John 14:20; Hebrews 13:5; Colossians 2:13-14; 1 John 5:13; Galatians 5:25*
- You commit yourself to God. *Colossians 2:6-7*

LEAD TO CHRIST
After you have explained the plan of salvation, there comes the moment of truth—when the young person actually prays to receive Christ. As you lead the person through this life-changing experience, remember the following.

Content
Explain that the prayer of faith is a personal conversation between a person and God. What is said is important, but what is meant is even more important. In other words, the young person should really mean what he or she says, not simply go through the motions by repeating a prayer after you.

To make it easy for the young person to remember and to

A VOICE

In the stillness,
I sat alone.
Hungry and cold.
Waiting to die,
Chained to my
Memories of the past,
While the darkness
Surrounded me.
I cried out for help,
But it was in vain.
For help never comes to
The unworthy.
There I sat,
Drowning in self-pity.
But then I heard a voice,
Echoing through the
Emptiness of my heart
This voice was calm,
Reassuring and trustworthy.
This voice spoke of love and—
Even of forgiveness.
How could this be?
I'm so undeserving.
Then the voice spoke again,
And I knew.
It said:
I died for you.

by Mona Lisa Currie
11th grade student
Covington, LA

emphasize the necessity for repentance, belief, trust, and commitment, explain that there are three basic parts to this prayer.

The first part says, in essence,"I'm sorry." This is where a person admits he or she has sinned . . . has lived for self, apart from God. The person is saying, "I'm sorry, God, for being self-centered and for breaking Your laws." This is *repentance,* the first step toward Christ.

The second part of the prayer says, in essence, "Thank you." Here the individual thanks God for sending Christ to die for his or her sins. This statement reinforces the facts of the Gospel.

The final portion of the prayer is the request, "Take over." When the young person says, "Come in and take over, Lord. I give my life to You," he or she is expressing trust and is making that personal commitment.

By uttering this simple prayer of faith, a young person enters into a new relationship with God, the Heavenly Father. He or she is born again and adopted into His family.

Although this seems easy enough, the last statement is often very difficult to say. I believe it is because this is the final moment of truth where the individual casts his or her fate on Christ, and this is where Satan attacks with doubts or fears. Be ready to encourage the young person at this point.

Process
In leading someone to Christ, I use a three prayer process.

First, I pray aloud, thanking God for the person and for what He is going to do in the individual's life and asking God to give him or her the courage to make this decision.

Second, the young person prays aloud, following the three-part format outlined above. I want him or her to pray aloud so that I can be a witness to this commitment. I also encourage the person to talk to God conversationally, using his own words.

Finally, I pray aloud, thanking God again for this young person and for what He has done.

However you choose to lead the young person, make sure that he knows what he's doing and why.

Follow-through
Afterward, it is important to make sure the person understands what just happened, the transaction which took place,

and the relationship which was formed. These questions will help.

• *"What did you just do?"* By asking this, you will help the person put the experience into his or her own words. He may say something like: "I just gave my life to Jesus!"

• *"What just happened to you?"* This question will build assurance that what happened was real and that God keeps His promises. It would be good to remind the person of 2 Corinthians 5:17, "Therefore, if anyone is in Christ, he is a new creation; the old has gone, the new has come!"

Tell him or her, "Whatever you feel like, He is there right now! You can trust God and His Word to be true."

First John 5:13 will also be helpful. "I write these things to you who believe in the name of the Son of God so that you may know that you have eternal life."

• *"How do you know you're a Christian?"* In discussing the answer to this question, you will have the opportunity to emphasize that the person's assurance should be based on facts, not on feelings. The fact is that God promises that He will come into someone's life when he or she repents and believes. It is also a fact that on this date at this time, this person prayed and made that personal commitment. You are there; you are a witness. No matter what happens, where the person is, or how he or she feels—no one can take that away. The fact is . . . he or she is a Christian, a child of God.

• *"Who would really like to know about what you just did?"* After the young person answers, encourage him or her to tell that person as soon as possible. This will be a tremendous encouragement to the new Christian and to the Christian friend, parent, or leader. It will also be the first opportunity for her to "confess Christ" to someone else.

In addition to walking the young person through these questions, be sure to give him or her some literature which will help him with initial questions and get him into the Word. "Your Most Important Relationship" lists steps to take "to keep growing in your relationship with God." (See the copy at the end of this chapter.)

A modern translation of the Bible is a necessity, especially if the young person doesn't own a Bible. And there are many booklets available from Christian publishers and organizations which can help the new believer through the first few steps of the faith.

It is also important to set up a time to see the young person again within 72 hours. At this time you can see how he or she has done in studying the booklet and in reading the Bible. At that time you can also answer any questions which may have arisen.

In chapter 11, we will discuss the discipleship process in more depth.

More than twenty-five years ago, while traveling on a Gospel team for Wheaton College, I had the privilege of praying with a young woman after one of our programs. I was a senior in college, and in that Christian environment, few were the opportunities to witness to unbelievers. Because I had not seen anyone respond for years, I had begun to doubt that it really "worked."

Carefully I explained what she had to do to "accept Christ as her personal Saviour," silently praying, "Please God, help Shelly, and show me that this is true."

We prayed together, and as she looked up, Shelly exclaimed, "It's different! God's real, and He's here!"

During the decades to follow, I have seen this repeated in scores of individual lives. Each person's response is his or her own, but the result is the same—God transforming a life and bringing another child into His Kingdom. What a privilege to be part of that process!

Bridges are for crossing. We must build strong, relational bridges with young people, making friendships, gaining their confidence, and winning the right to be heard. But we must also be ready to cross those bridges with a clear presentation of the life-changing message of Christ.

YOU were created with value and worth.
God wants your life to count.

Did you know . . .

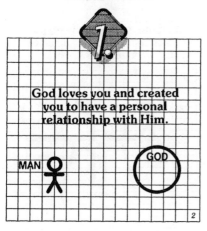

God loves you and created you to have a personal relationship with Him.

MAN   GOD

2

God created you.
In Psalm 139:13-14 the Bible says, "You made all the delicate, inner parts of my body, and knit them together in my mother's womb. Thank you for making me so wonderfully complex!"

God loves you.
"For God loved the world so much that he gave his only Son so that anyone who believes in him shall not perish but have eternal life." (John 3:16)

God wants you to know him.
"And this is the way to have eternal life — by knowing you, the only true God, and Jesus Christ, the one you sent to earth!" (John 17:3)

Why is it that many people do not have a personal relationship with God? 3

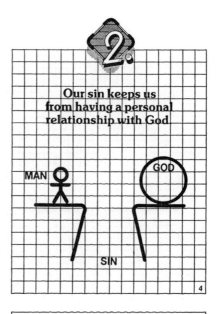

Our sin keeps us from having a personal relationship with God

MAN   GOD

SIN

4

What is sin?
"Knowing what is right to do and then not doing it is sin." (James 4:17) You see, God is holy and perfect . . . and we are not. Sin not only means doing wrong or failing to do all that God wants. Sin is also our attitude of ignoring or rejecting God. Because God is holy, he cannot accept our sin.

Who has sinned?
"Yes, they all have sinned; all fall short of God's glorious ideal ; . . ." (Romans 3:23)

What happens when we sin?
"But the trouble is that your sins have cut you off from God." (Isaiah 59:2) "For the wages of sin is death." (Romans 6:23) Sin causes a gap between God and us. Death, which means eternal separation from God, is the penalty of our sin.

5

What is the solution to our separation from God?

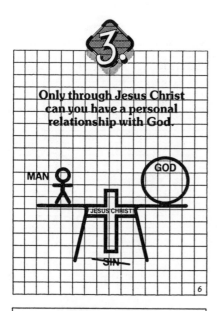

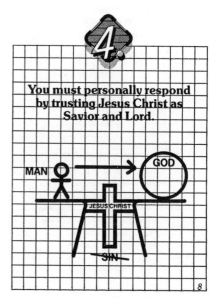

Why Jesus Christ?

In John 14:6 Jesus said, "I am the Way – yes, and the Truth and the Life. No one can get to the Father except by means of me." It is only through Jesus Christ that we can have a relationship with God.

Why did Jesus Christ have to die?

"He died once for the sins of all us guilty sinners, although he himself was innocent of any sin at any time, that he might bring us safely home to God." (1 Peter 3:18) Jesus died to pay the penalty for our sins, so we might be forgiven.

Why did Christ rise from the dead?

Jesus Christ rose from the dead to prove he could give us eternal life. "Christ died for our sins just as the Scriptures said he would . . . he was buried . . . three days afterwards he arose from the grave just as the prophets foretold . . . he was seen by more than five hundred Christian brothers at one time . . ." (1 Corinthians 15:3-6)

7

How can you begin your personal relationship with God?

You respond with trust in Christ.

In Ephesians 2:8-9 the Bible says, "Because of his kindness you have been saved through trusting Christ. And even trusting is not of yourselves; it too is a gift from God. Salvation is not a reward for the good we have done, so none of us can take any credit for it."

You respond by turning to God from sin.

"Now change your mind and attitude to God and turn to him so he can cleanse away your sins . . . ." (Acts 3:19)

You respond by receiving Christ.

"To all who received him, he gave the right to become children of God. All they needed to do was to trust him to save them." (John 1:12) Receiving Christ means:
• Turning to God from your own way of living (repentance).
• Inviting Christ to come into your life and trusting him to forgive your sin.
• Allowing God to direct your life.
  Receiving Jesus Christ is not just an emotional experience; nor is it just agreeing with your mind that Jesus is the Son of God. It means *total trust*, an act of your will.

9

What about you?

Where would you place yourself in this illustration?

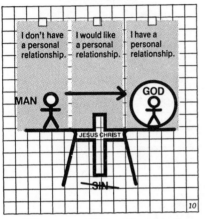

Where would you like to be?

You can begin your personal
relationship with God
by receiving Jesus Christ by faith.

You can express your faith (trust) through prayer.
Prayer is simply talking to God. He knows what you
mean even when it is difficult to express yourself.
You may use the following words or your own.

"Dear God, I know that my sin has
separated me from you. Thank you
that Jesus Christ died in my place.
I ask Jesus to forgive my sin and
to come into my life. Please begin
to direct my life. Thank you for
giving me eternal life. In Jesus'
name, Amen."

Can you say this to God, and mean it?
If you can, pray right now and trust Jesus to forgive
your sin and come into your life, as he promised.

11

What's next?

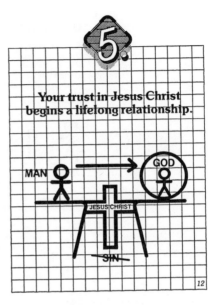

**Your trust in Jesus Christ
begins a lifelong relationship.**

12

God commits himself to you.

- God assures you that Jesus Christ has come into
  your life. In John 14:20 Jesus says, ". . . I am in
  my Father, and you in me, and I in you."
- God will never leave you. "I will never, *never*
  fail you nor forsake you." (Hebrews 13:5)
- God completely forgives your sin. "For he for-
  gave all your sins, and blotted out the
  charges proved against you." (Colossians
  2:13-14)
- God assures you that you have eternal life. "I
  have written this to you who believe in the
  Son of God so you may know that you have
  eternal life." (1 John 5:13)
- God gives you his Holy Spirit to enable you to live
  the Christian life. "Let us follow the Holy
  Spirit's leading in every part of our lives."
  (Galatians 5:25)

*Wouldn't you like to stop and thank God that
Christ is in your life and will never leave you?*

You commit yourself to God.

In Colossians 2:6-7 the Bible says, "And now just
as you trusted Christ to save you, trust him,
too, for each day's problems ; . . See that you
go on growing in the Lord, and become strong
and vigorous . . . ."

13

Do not depend upon feelings.

No matter how you feel. God always remains committed to you. The promises in God's Word. the Bible. are your authority. This illustration shows the relationship between **fact** (God and his Word). **faith** (our trust in God and his Word) and our **feelings**.

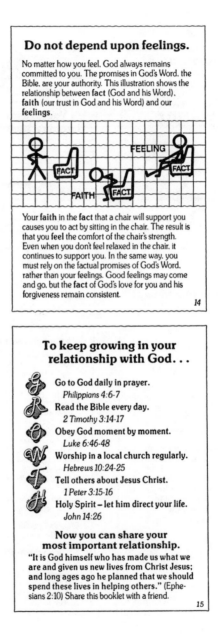

Your **faith** in the **fact** that a chair will support you causes you to act by sitting in the chair. The result is that you **feel** the comfort of the chair's strength. Even when you don't feel relaxed in the chair. it continues to support you. In the same way. you must rely on the factual promises of God's Word. rather than your feelings. Good feelings may come and go. but the **fact** of God's love for you and his forgiveness remain consistent.

14

To keep growing in your relationship with God...

Go to God daily in prayer.
Philippians 4:6-7

Read the Bible every day.
2 Timothy 3:14-17

Obey God moment by moment.
Luke 6:46-48

Worship in a local church regularly.
Hebrews 10:24-25

Tell others about Jesus Christ.
1 Peter 3:15-16

Holy Spirit – let him direct your life.
John 14:26

Now you can share your most important relationship.

"It is God himself who has made us what we are and given us new lives from Christ Jesus; and long ages ago he planned that we should spend these lives in helping others." (Ephesians 2:10) Share this booklet with a friend.

15

CHAPTER NINE

Togetherness

His 6-foot 4-inch, 250-pound frame filled the doorway and cast an imposing shadow. Quickly surveying the others gathered there, Brad strode into the room and dropped into the La-Z-Boy in the corner. The "whoosh" of escaping air from the chair was covered by comments of "How's the shoulder?" "Great game Friday," and assorted compliments and greetings. A few seconds later, Gene made his entrance. Tall and gangly, Gene's play at split end was improving rapidly. In fact, his touchdown catch had proven to be the game-winner.

Tossing verbal quips and smiles to the rest of the group, Gene found a chair and pulled it into the circle which included five other members of the high school football team.

On the other side of the room, the kitchen door swung open as Ted Dwyer emerged carrying a huge bowl of popcorn. Following close behind was Sally, Ted's wife, with a tray of soft drinks and napkins.

Large hands plunged eagerly into the popcorn and carried fistfuls to laps and mouths, and Ted began: "Hey, it's great to see you again. Gordon couldn't make it tonight, so this is everyone. I appreciate you guys being here, and I hope you find these discussions interesting. I know that I've been learning a lot. Anyway, last week we looked at the first two chapters. Do any of you have any questions about what we read or discussed?" Pulling out the Gospels and laying them on the table, Ted continued to lead the discussion.

During the summer, Ted had begun jogging after work at the high school stadium. There he had met Brad, Gene, Gordon, and the others, working out for the upcoming football season. Having played quarterback in college, Ted offered to throw passes and to give tips to the quarterback and receivers in the group. For the next two weeks (before official practice with the coaches began), Ted spent a couple of hours a day playing ball with these young athletes and getting to know them personally. And they jumped at the chance to go to the first NFL preseason game when Ted got the tickets.

After the formal practices began, Ted would attend their workouts and scrimmages when his schedule allowed. And once or twice, he had some of the guys over for pizza while they watched Monday Night Football together.

The transition from football to friendship and from tackling to talking was smooth as they began to know and respect each other. As a concerned Christian layman, Ted wanted to share the Gospel with these young men, but he wasn't sure how. Then he discovered that one of the boys was also a Christian.

Soon Paul, the Christian athlete, Paul's parents, and Ted met and decided together to design an evangelism strategy. Their prayers and plans led them to begin a short study of the Gospel of Mark, "to see what Jesus was really like." Because they liked Ted, the young athletes agreed to meet on Monday nights, just before the televised game, for six weeks.

Each week, the hour passed quickly, packed with provocative questions and animated answers. Most of the boys had never read a Bible they could understand, and they had a variety of misconceptions about God and Jesus.

During the weeks that followed, Ted was able to present a

clear picture of God's Son and of how to become His follow-ers. As a result, two of his young athlete-friends made that life-changing commitment, and the others promised to give it serious consideration.

SMALL GROUPS

Using small groups can be an effective strategy for building relationships and communicating the Gospel to young people. In certain situations, it can be a very effective evangelistic tool. There may be debate over the optimum size for these groups, but for our purposes, a small group consists of four to eight people, including the leader.

Obviously, the most effective communication of any mes-sage takes place one-on-one, person-to-person, where individ-uals are free to express their true feelings and questions, to be vulnerable, and to ask for help. Also, in individual counseling sessions, there is more freedom to confront and to ask difficult questions which would be embarrassing in front of others in a group.

But there are times when small groups will be more appro-priate and effective than immediate, individual attention. Meeting as a group has advantages.

Small Group Advantage #1

Young people like to do things together . . . in groups. This characteristic, which also leads to peer pressure and cliques, can be put to good use as a bridge for the Gospel. If certain kids want to do something, others will follow and join the group. The expressions, "Everybody's going!" and "Every-one's doing it!" have their origins in the need for adolescents to be accepted, belong, and be part of "the group."

Small Group Advantage #2

A group is socially acceptable. Often friends and/or parents will question the motives of an adult who hangs around and gives a lot of attention to a certain boy or girl. But if a *group* of kids is involved, those questions rarely arise, especially when the adult sponsor is a neighbor, coach, teacher, or parent of another student.

Groups come in different sizes and shapes. There are activity groups. If a person has ever played on an athletic team, that is a group. There are sensitivity groups where people get together and relate gut-level feelings. A therapy group is where people get together to deal with an unconscious conflict or to take a deep introspective look at themselves. Natural friendship groups are groups of people who have inclinations and things in common, and get together after school or over a Coke. They're friends. There are problem-solving groups where people who have particular questions about a certain topic are looking for answers. This kind of group is very content oriented. Certainly there are teaching and classroom groups that would fit in this category.

From *The Whole Person Survival Kit*, Art Deyo, Ed. (Youth for Christ International, Wheaton, Ill. 1976).

Small Group Advantage #3

There are some activities which only small groups can do. It would be nearly impossible to play volleyball with just one or two people or to run a relay. Small groups are ideal for playing board games or card games, singing, discussing, brainstorming, constructing, telling jokes, and so forth. And many activities such as cheering at games, swimming, jogging, watching movies, and others are enhanced by group interaction.

Small Group Advantage #4

Small groups can provide opportunities for communication. A shy young person may not feel free to express his or her feelings individually or in a group. But after hearing another person verbalize what *he* is feeling, he will listen very carefully to your answer. Or someone in the group may propose an idea or ask a question which sheds new light on the subject—

perhaps even a thought that you may not have considered. Often kids will be more willing to learn from each other than from an adult. And the creative tension of opposing viewpoints helps young people think through the implications of an intellectual position or a lifestyle.

The group experience may also open new lines of communication between and among group members—it may be a way of bringing people together.

While there are many advantages to the small-group approach, it is important to be aware of several disadvantages in dealing with small groups. These potential problems tend to center around group dynamics.

Small Group Disadvantage #1

Relationships multiply rapidly. With two people, there is only one relationship on which to work and about which to be concerned. Add one more person, and suddenly four relationships are involved, each combination of two and the three people together. If you doubt this, watch what happens when you introduce a child to a couple of children in a playroom.

Four people in a group provides ten possible relationships (all the combinations of two, three, and four). The multiplication continues with each new member. In other words, each group will have its own personality and feel depending on who's there. The changing environment of group dynamics can present special challenges.

Small Group Disadvantage #2

Personalities often clash. Do you remember the Sunday School class with that person who just seemed to rub you the wrong way? You two could never hit it off. In any group, there is the strong possibility of conflicting personalities—two people who don't get along and who argue over everything. This can make a positive group chemistry virtually impossible.

Small Group Disadvantage #3

Individuals can sometimes dominate or intimidate. One of the goals of a small group experience is to make the members feel welcome, accepted, and free to express themselves. Often, however, one or two people will dominate the discussion or so dogmatically state their positions that others are afraid to respond.

Small Group Disadvantage #4

People play social "games." If someone is in a bad mood, he or she might say something critical, judgmental, or shocking just to get a rise from others. Or when someone wants to make an impression, he may be less than honest with his true thoughts and feelings. Verbal, social games are often played to get attention, flirt, or hurt someone.

It is important to remember these possible malfunctions in group dynamics and to minimize their effects. Ideas on how to counteract small group disadvantages will be presented later in this chapter.

PURPOSE

Over the years, small groups have been organized for a variety of reasons, including planning, teaching, counseling, problem-solving, and others. Because our ultimate purpose in developing small groups is to communicate the Gospel, we will focus on how small groups can build relationships and help you teach young people about Christ. Later, in chapter 11, we will discuss using small groups to help new Christians grow in their faith.

Building Relationships

As was the case with Ted Dwyer and his athlete associates, small groups can be an excellent way to develop friendships with young people. This band of guys centered their time around football—playing, watching, discussing. Soon the group itself became more important than the activity—the guys just enjoyed being together. Ted and Paul were then able to move the guys in the group into a regular discussion of the Bible.

As you think through your evangelism strategy, consider the *group* as well as the *individual*. You may find it is harder to get one person to participate with you and easier to get a few group members involved in the activity.

SMALL-GROUP SUGGESTIONS

1. *The group must meet the needs of individuals.* The teenager sees something in it for himself.
2. *Groups must be based on common interests.* For example, a group of girls may want to meet regularly to talk over family and boy problems, seeking solutions from the Bible. This is an area of common interest that can draw the group together.
3. *Groups should have some diversity in personality* in order to enhance group interaction. Don't put eight kids who have all been charged with assault and battery in one group. Nor should all members of a group be quiet and withdrawn. You may end up as a leader of a meditation group.
4. *The group should gain a commitment from the guys or girls to be a part of the group.* If a person feels forced into a small group, then he will most likely come late, skip meetings, or say at a later date, "I didn't want to be a part of this group anyway." If it's his choice and he commits himself to the others, he carries responsibility for the success of the group. You become a facilitator, not a group "owner."
5. *The group has to be safe.* If you're in a group and one kid begins attacking another with very rude and vicious comments, the leader has the responsibility to step in and protect the person from being hurt. Don't cut off the feelings that have been expressed, but help the members discuss feelings about others without letting them attack each other's characters.
6. *The time and place of group meetings needs to be very clearly understood.* Don't assume anything. When setting up a group meeting, make sure it is very clear where the meeting is to be held, what time, and how transportation is being arranged.

The Whole Person Survival Kit, edited by Art Deyo. (Wheaton, Ill.: Youth For Christ International, 1976).

Communicating the Gospel
Eventually, of course, we want to be able to share Christ with these young men and women. This goal should always be in the back of our minds as we plan and participate in a small group. This means praying continually for the opportunity to get serious, go deeper, or turn the corner in a group discussion.

FORMING THE GROUP
Because of the advantages and disadvantages of small groups which were discussed earlier, it is important to remember the following points when forming a group.

First, if possible choose *all girls* or *all guys*. You can have a successful mixed group, but often the presence of the opposite sex can create havoc with group dynamics as boys and girls try to impress each other or guard what they say. And if they have dated before, innuendos, jokes, and subtle insults will often fly.

Second, center the group around a common interest. Football was the obvious interest of Ted's group, during the football season. But in two months, another sport could dominate the attention of certain group members. The common interest, therefore, does not have to be long term. By choosing carefully the interest or subject, you will have the attention and enthusiastic involvement of specific kids.

I have a friend who loves to hunt and fish, and he is quite proficient at both. Every year, he finds high school guys with the same interest who would love to join him on a trip. Another friend is a "Jazzercize" instructor. One spring, she gathered a group of high school girls together for regular workouts and discussions.

Beginning with the common interest, you will be able to develop friendships with group members. Then, individually or in the group, you can suggest doing something else together . . . like studying the Bible or the life of Christ.

Third, begin with a felt need. This is similar to a common interest and is an alternative. There may be a subject that a group of kids would *want* to discuss. In other words, because of recent events or their own pressing feelings and personal experiences, young people have questions which are crying for answers. This can be a great opportunity to begin a dynamic small group.

Junior high girls and almost *all* high schoolers want to talk about dating and sex. I have known many adults who have centered group discussions around this topic. Junior high boys want to learn how to improve at a particular sport or activity because of their growing and changing bodies and their need to prove their masculinity.

A number of years ago, a sophomore cheerleader was killed on her way to Florida for spring vacation. Because the family had left early for the trip, school was still in session; the whole school had heard about the tragedy. Kids stood in stunned silence or whispered in the halls when the news broke, and many, for the first time in their young lives, began to think seriously about death, dying, and their reason for living. This was a felt need. At our Campus Life meeting that night, we switched gears. Instead of the games and scheduled discussion and wrap-up, we held a memorial service for Linda. Many of her friends attended. Because of that meeting and subsequent contacts, I know of at least five young men who became Christians.

Other felt needs could include suicide, loneliness, family, the future, dealing with divorce, etc. If kids feel it, they will be interested.

Finally, look for natural groupings. Be careful not to put together a group of strangers. In extreme cases, all of the group dynamics problems will occur, the meeting will be a disaster, and you probably won't meet more than once or twice. Instead, work with a group of friends or with those who have as much in common as possible. A group of sophomore boys, for example, would be good, especially if they already know each other . . . or the upperclassmen girls who enjoy drama. I'm sure you can think of other possibilities. The closer you can come to the same sex, age, interests, and friendship, the better will be your chances of success. Note: A coed group can be effective if it is a natural grouping, such as a group of friends. In fact certain YFC chapters are testing this approach as an evangelistic strategy for their communities.

For more information contact Dave Bartlett, Backbone Area YFC, P.O. Box 59, Manchester, IA 52057 (319) 927-6569.

Building Relationships with Guys
This list is by no means exhaustive, but it can be a catalyst for your creative thinking. Some of the activities and topics which should interest young men are:
● participating in team sports—football, basketball, baseball, rugby, volleyball, soccer, etc.
● participating in individual sports—tennis, swimming, running, jogging, fishing, hunting, sailing, skateboarding, surfing, skiing, etc.
● watching the sport of their interest (in person or on television)—pro or college games, 10Ks, marathons, car or motorcycle races, college or pro meets and tournaments, pro practices, pro exhibitions
● working with computers
● watching and reviewing movies and videos
● performing and listening to popular music
● working with their hands—carpentry, woodworking, car repairing, etc.
● talking about girls—dating, marriage, sex
● learning about leadership

Building Relationships with Girls
Some of the activities and topics which should interest young women are:
● participating in team sports—soccer, volleyball, field hockey, basketball, softball, etc.
● participating in individual sports—tennis, swimming, skiing, skating, sailing, surfing, running, Jazzercize, etc.
● watching the sport of their interest (in person or on television)—college or pro games and cheerleaders, 10Ks, marathons, college or pro meets and tournaments, pro exhibitions
● watching and reviewing movies and videos
● performing and listening to music
● shopping
● learning about fashion and interior design
● learning craft

- talking about boys—friendship, dating, marriage, sex
- discussing the future or family
- reading and discussing a book

GETTING STARTED

There is no "correct" way to form a group or to get together. Just look for the opportunity to suggest that you all do something together. Or, like Ted Dwyer, build a minitradition. Then, if there is a felt need or if you feel the time is right, suggest getting together on a regular basis to discuss life, problems, or a certain subject.

Topics for Discussion

The "life of Christ" would be an excellent topic for discussion. Choose about six scenes from His life, one for each week, around which to center your discussion. These scenes should give a total picture of the real Jesus and could include: His birth; the discussion with the temple elders and the description in Luke 2:52 of His teenage years; the temptations in the wilderness; His throwing the money changers out of the temple; illustrations of His compassion through healing lepers and others, feeding the hungry, and raising the dead; and His death, burial, and resurrection.

Another possibility would be to discuss "Your Most Important Relationship." Each week you could go through one point of the booklet described in chapter 7.

There are many booklets, books, and videos available from your Christian bookstore which would be excellent resources. Some of the ones which I have used are "Breaking Free," "Stop, Look, Listen, Go," and "How to Get What You Need" from Youth for Christ (available from YFC Sales—312-668-6600).These were written with early adolescents and troubled youth in mind.

The Campus Life Books (published by Tyndale House) are also very good. *Do You Sometimes Feel Like a Nobody?* is about self-esteem, *A Love Story* discusses love and sex, and *Just One Victory* deals with drinking. And for Bible studies, check out Mark or Genesis of the Life Application Bible series from Tyndale House or *The Student Bible* from Zondervan.

First Meeting
The first time you get together as a group to discuss or to talk seriously, it is important to cover the following points. This will help the group function smoothly.

• *Length*—Explain that you will be meeting for only six or seven weeks (depending on the time available). After that, you will decide as a group whether to continue to meet.

• *Time and Place*—Decide on a regular meeting place and time. You can move from week to week, but consistency is best. You could meet in a home or a restaurant, in the mornings, after school, or evenings. One group called themselves "The Breakfast Club," and they met every Friday morning, before school, for breakfast at McDonald's.

• *Ground Rules*—Outline what you expect of the group and what they can expect from you. This includes attendance (everyone should plan to be at every meeting), the length of each session (one hour, not including any activity or refreshments), preparation, and discussion guidelines (see below under "teach").

• *Names and Numbers*—Distribute a piece of paper and have group members write their names and phone numbers. Later, type the sheet and give each person a copy so thay can contact anyone if they need help or just want to talk. Be sure to have your own name and number on the sheet.

THE PROCESS
As with "initiating relationships" (chapter 4), "building relationships" (chapter 5), and "appointments with individuals" (chapter 6), organizing and leading small groups involves a four-step process. The steps are *plan, coordinate, teach,* and *assess.*

Step #1—Plan
This step requires you to decide who should be in the group and what you will discuss. It also means you should be praying for the success of your group, before you get started and before each meeting. Use the "Small Group Preparation" sheet printed at the end of this chapter as a planning guide.

Because small groups involve young people and are discus-

SMALL GROUP PROCESS

The Boston model of group process says that all groups move through four basic stages.

1. *The first stage is inclusion.* When a young person enters a new setting where there is more than one person, one of the first questions that he asks himself is, "Do I want to be a part of this?" "Who are these people?" "What do they want?" "What's in this for me?" If a leader can successfully deal with inclusion it's possible to facilitate increased group growth.
2. *The second stage is control.* This is the stage where people are saying, "Who's in charge here?" "Who controls the decision-making process?" "Who runs the discussion?" "Do I accept the authority?" Of course, a group doesn't corporately say, "I feel wanted, so let's move into control. Now I think I'll challenge the leader." Group process is not a mechanical system of change. Everybody moves into the group experience at various levels. The sensitive leader will include others in various parts of the group experience so that they may feel that the "controller" is responsive to them.
3. *The third stage is closeness*—the stage into which a group moves when persons feel completely comfortable with others. The group participants like being around each other, and accept the leadership roles within the group.
4. *Separation is the final stage.* A lot of kids are going to have trouble facing separation, especially if they have become part of an intimate group. One way to deal with separation is to let the group know from the start how long it is going to last. Set a time limit on the life of the group. At the end of that time let the group decide whether or not it wants to make a contract for a longer period of time.

The Whole Person Survival Kit, edited by Art Deyo. (Wheaton, Ill.: Youth For Christ International, 1976).

sion oriented, there will be great spontaneity. You may end up discussing something completely different than what you had planned. This doesn't mean you shouldn't be prepared. Your role is to guide the group, to facilitate discussion, and to answer questions. Therefore, each small group meeting should be carefully planned in the sense that you are ready for just about anything—to teach the specified content, to troubleshoot, or to answer questions.

"Planning" also involves an alternate plan if new kids come or if hardly anyone shows up. When you and the host are the only ones there, it could be the perfect opportunity to really get to know him or to share the Gospel with him.

Step #2—Coordinate

This step involves communicating with group members, letting them know the schedule and of any changes and reminding them of meetings and other activities.

Coordinating also means checking with parents, preparing the meeting place, and looking over the schedule in advance to head off any conflicts with school activities, vacations, etc. Remember, however, that a day off school can be a great time for a special group activity.

Step #3—Teach

During the meeting, it is important to be the leader *and* a participant. In other words, you have to take charge, set the tone, and bring the "content" to the meeting. But you also should take the role of a fellow learner. Here are some guidelines for leading and teaching in a small group.

1. Set up the physical surroundings, prevent distractions, and get the interaction started.

2. Help kids feel that they are understood, welcome, and accepted as they are.

3. Encourage everyone to talk about himself or herself.

4. Don't waste time on theoretical or nonsense subjects.

5. Always keep listening.

6. Always keep digging to root causes and real feelings.

7. Try to avoid answering questions (like the "answer man"); instead, throw the question back to the group through

DISCUSSION HELPERS

When you suspect that the speaker has no evidence . . . "Why do you believe that?" "What have you observed that makes you think so?" (Perhaps, if he *does* come up with an example, you may agree with him.)

When you feel yourself getting upset and you don't know why . . . "Is anyone else uneasy about all this?" "Does anyone feel disturbed or confused?" (Perhaps others can explain what you're sensing.)

When you can't believe what you're hearing . . . "Do I understand what you're saying—correct me if I don't" and then go on to carefully restate what you think he said.

When an interesting point has been lost in the shuffle . . . "Could we go back to something that was said earlier?" "Could we go into this a little more?" You can encourage a speaker without committing yourself to his position.

When a speaker is giving lots of examples, but you suspect a far-out conclusion . . . "I agree with your facts, but toward what point are you heading?" (This avoids putting words in his mouth.)

When everyone is hung up on a detail . . . "I think I've lost the track. How did we get to this point?"

from *Concern: High School Discussion Series*, Silver-Burdette Co.

more questions so that eventually they will come up with their own answers.

8. Be alert to hidden agendas—preoccupations which keep

members from concentrating on the subject.

9. Stay flexible.

It is also important to explain and police your discussion guidelines. Here are some possible ground rules for the *whole group* to follow.

1. Outside the group, keep quiet about what happens or what is said inside the group, especially when someone has shared something very personal.

2. Don't try to impress the others with your strengths or weaknesses.

3. Be honest enough to tell the other person how you feel about him or her.

4. Don't insist that everybody should think like you do, or get offended when someone disagrees with you.

5. Try to see things from the other person's point of view.

6. Avoid value judgments and labeling.

7. Never assume that you know all about what others are talking about.

8. Don't talk too much or too little.

9. Don't be afraid to become a true friend.

Step #4—Assess

After each meeting evaluate how it went, your leadership, input, and responses, and the comments of each participant. And think through how you could improve the small group. This also means checking with group members on how they are doing with an assignment you gave or with a specific area of their lives which they may have shared in the meeting. Use the "Small Group Evaluation" sheet printed at the end of the chapter.

After the six weeks, it is important to have a group assessment. Give them the opportunity to evaluate the group and to offer suggestions for improvement. They should also decide whether or not they want to meet for another six weeks. If, in the course of your meetings, some of the group members have made personal commitments to Christ, their next group experience could involve material to help them grow in their new faith.

Small groups can be a very effective way to build relationships with young people and to communicate the Gospel. Look for natural groupings with whom you already have the beginnings of friendships. Get involved with them informally in an activity. Then organize these friends into a small group to learn together. Use small groups as a bridge to Christ.

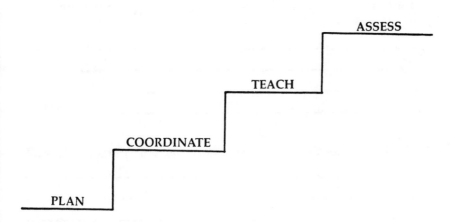

Small-Group Preparation

Specific Questions Regarding Your Group

1. What are their specific interests or felt needs; i.e., what the students perceive as their needs, even though those may not be their real needs?

---

2. What are the students' real needs as you perceive them?

---

3. What is the most effective strategy for meeting their needs and capturing their interests?

---

4. What are some *measurable* goals you can set to help meet their felt and real needs?

Small-Group Evaluation

Review Questions to Determine Progress of the Group

1. How is the group progressing in achieving its goals, felt and real needs?

_____

_____

_____

2. Is personal initiative taking place in growth toward evangelism?

name	observations
name	observations
name	observations
name	observations
name	observations
name	observations

3. How are the group dynamics developing? (interpersonal relationships, sharing together) Do you sense conflict in the group? Is it being resolved? Are there any changes needed?

_____

_____

_____

4. Are participants following through with assignments? (You may need to contact them during the week to see how they are doing on their assignments.)

_____

_____

CHAPTER TEN

The Big Event

Laughter and cheers fill the house and then subside as about a hundred young people eagerly await the next *crowd-breaker*. "And now," announces the emcee, "we're going to have a battle between the sexes, testing reflexes and coordination. Representing the *women* of South High School is Marlene!" A deafening cheer rises from the female half of the overfilled family room.

Continuing with the introductions, the leader shouts, "And representing the *men* is Rob!"

"Go Rob! Go Rob! Go Rob!" chant the guys in response as Marlene and Rob wade through the sea of bodies to the front of the room.

After a brief explanation to competitors and crowd, the contest begins in earnest with both sides cheering their worthy representatives.

Afterward, the focus turns to a lively discussion of the evening's topic with a rainbow of opinions expressed. About ten minutes later, the leader wraps up the meeting, giving helpful advice on the subject at hand and explaining how God is vitally concerned with this area of their lives. He also challenges them to be open to a relationship with Christ, and he suggests that they check the appropriate place on their "react cards" if they want to get together to talk about it. Then he reminds them of future events and sends them to the refreshments.

It's a Campus Life meeting for South High—a place where young people can be accepted, have fun, meet others, and receive answers to life's most important questions. Kids come to the meetings because "everyone's there" and because they enjoy the program. But most of all, they come because of relationships they have with the Campus Life staff members, volunteers, and student leaders.

Meetings such as this can provide excellent opportunities for responsible and effective communication of the Gospel. As stated in chapter 4, one of the New Testament principles of evangelism is "maximum influence." This means spreading the Good News to as many people as possible. Drawing and speaking to crowds is one way to do just that.

A Word of Warning
Before discussing this further, however, it is important to remember that large meetings do not happen automatically or easily, especially when trying to break through the clutter in the marketplace (see chapter 2) to reach the vast audience of kids untouched by a Christian church or organization. We shouldn't just book a speaker, rent an auditorium, and expect it to be packed out with young people. Believe me, they will stay away in droves.

And we should also understand that planning, programming, and pulling off successful meetings takes a lot of work. Before beginning this venture, we should count the cost in time, energy, and money.

A BIG EVENT PROVIDES OPPORTUNITY
We can have a very effective ministry with young people by

President Grover Cleveland was once asked, "How long would it take you to prepare a ten-minute address?"

"Three days," was his answer.

The interviewer was startled. "What happens when you have to speak for half an hour?" he asked.

"I can be ready for that in an afternoon," replied the President.

"What if you're given an hour and a half or two hours for a full oration?"

Cleveland smiled and answered, "I'm ready now!"

establishing friendships, one by one, and through small groups. We don't *need* large programs to reach youth for Christ.

On the other hand, given the right resources and climate, special events and meetings can expand the ministry considerably.

Ingredients

The necessary ingredients for running a successful large-group program include a network of other adults who are working with young people (in the same area and age-group), a broad base of contacts and relationships with students, the feeling by kids that they want to get together and that "there's nothing to do in this town," community support (school administration, parents, newspapers, etc.), places to meet, and people to organize and run the programs.

Advantages

There are certain advantages in using large meetings as a vehicle for evangelism. First, there is something special that happens in a large group setting when everyone is laughing, cheering, listening, and thinking together. Some activities, for example, can only be done successfully in a large group. The "wave cheer" has become popular at major sporting events. Thousands of fans stand, lift their arms, and scream on cue as the wave circles the stadium. Can you imagine trying that with a group of ten? Or how would a sing-along go over with a handful in the room? Many crowd-breakers, songs, discussions, informal polls, jokes, games, and talks work best in a crowd.

The fact that so many kids have gathered to hear someone sing or talk about God can remove a major stumbling block for faith in Christ. Kids are encouraged when they learn that many of their friends already follow Him.

A large group has the financial resources to attract and pay for a high-quality program. Professional speakers and musicians perform for their livelihood, and so they aren't cheap. Even films are expensive to rent. By dividing the costs among a large number of kids, you can afford to buy props, rent facilities, and hire outstanding communicators.

There are also human resources available in a large group. Volunteer adults and students can help gather materials, construct sets, distribute publicity, participate in programs, and run meetings.

Disadvantages
The disadvantages of large meetings and events include complexity. Planning, arranging, coordinating, and following through with a large event involve a myriad of details in lining up the facilities, program, and personnel; managing the budget; and handling crowd control. The more ambitious the project, the more complex it becomes. Hosting a miniconcert by a singer with her guitar in your living room is one thing; promoting a concert by an all-electric rock group in an auditorium is quite another.

Any successful program takes a significant investment of energy, time, and often money. Even Sunday School classes and small group discussions involve hours of preparation. A larger program or event will consume more time and energy, especially from the leader.

Special events, activities, and meetings can provide excellent opportunities to tell young people about Christ. But it is important to know what's involved before jumping in headfirst.

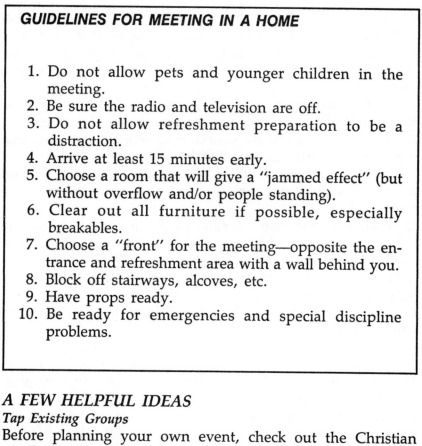

GUIDELINES FOR MEETING IN A HOME

1. Do not allow pets and younger children in the meeting.
2. Be sure the radio and television are off.
3. Do not allow refreshment preparation to be a distraction.
4. Arrive at least 15 minutes early.
5. Choose a room that will give a "jammed effect" (but without overflow and/or people standing).
6. Clear out all furniture if possible, especially breakables.
7. Choose a "front" for the meeting—opposite the entrance and refreshment area with a wall behind you.
8. Block off stairways, alcoves, etc.
9. Have props ready.
10. Be ready for emergencies and special discipline problems.

A FEW HELPFUL IDEAS

Tap Existing Groups

Before planning your own event, check out the Christian youth groups in your community. You could plug into their activities when appropriate; most of them would welcome your involvement.

Jack and Georgia were volunteer junior high sponsors at their church. Although the group was small for this young church, their daughter Emily was enjoying the group and had brought a couple of her friends from school to some meetings. Through other Christian parents, Jack and Georgia learned that the local Youth for Christ chapter was sponsoring area-wide events for junior highers every six weeks. The purpose of these activities was to pull together their Campus Life/JV clubs for an evening of high-energy games, music, and a special speaker. They also learned that YFC welcomed church groups to attend. After discussing the situation with Emily, they invited and brought a van load of her friends from church and school to the next area-wide event.

Youth for Christ (through the Campus Life and Campus Life/JV programs), Young Life, Fellowship of Christian Athletes, and other evangelical youth organizations will sponsor many meetings, rallies, concerts, competitions, conferences, retreats, and trips during the year. Because the purpose of these groups is *evangelism*, each of these programs will be geared to effective communication of the Gospel. And because these organizations aren't affiliated with one particular church or denomination, your young friends won't be threatened or turned off.

There are also many local church youth groups which will sponsor special concerts, speakers, or films. If these programs are held in a neutral setting, they may also provide a positive witness.

If you choose to attend programs sponsored by others, be sure to communicate with the leaders beforehand. Ask about their philosophy of ministry, what will happen in the program, what kind of a response will be requested, how they feel about your participation, and how you can help make the event successful.

Utilize Existing Networks
Many communities have an active association of youth ministers. Take your concerns and ideas to them and brainstorm together ideas for effective outreaches. One group you may wish to contact is the National Network of Youth Ministries (17150 Via Del Campo, Suite 102, San Diego, CA 92127). This group has been structured to help youth workers pool their resources and they can put you in touch with other members in your region.

Another network is other Christian adults who have a real heart for seeing kids come to Christ. Host a meeting of these like-minded folks and plan together. The Youth for Christ ministry to junior highers (Campus Life/JV), for example, is built around volunteer teams of concerned Christian parents—each school or neighborhood club is organized and run by them. And many high school Campus Life and Young Life clubs are led by volunteers. Fellowship of Christian Athletes "huddle" groups are led by coaches, teachers, or other adults in the community. The idea is to build a base of adult support and work together.

Christian young people should be challenged to reach other kids for Christ. We will discuss this further in chapter 12. The point is that you can pull together the Christian young people you know and plan a special outreach event together. If you are a parent, begin with your son or daughter. Expand the group to include kids from church and other Christian young people in the neighborhood and school. Then host a meeting and ask them what they think would be an effective way to attract and reach their non-Christian friends.

Sponsor Assembly Programs

Taking the microphone, the sandy-haired young man issues a challenge. "Send me your best Ping-Pong player. I'd like to play him or her a quick game."

A few seconds later, as the curtain is pulled back to reveal a table and paddles, a lanky student is pulled from his seat in the packed auditorium. With an embarrassed shrug of his shoulders and a wave to his volunteering friends, he climbs the stairs to the stage.

Soon the game begins, with the usual spins, slams, and hollow plastic sounds of the ball hitting the table. With each point, the audience cheers, but more for the visitor than for their fellow student. And then it's over—a close game with the student on the short end of the score. Quickly the auditorium falls silent as Skip rolls back to the mike and begins to speak. He talks about his past, especially of his days as an outstanding high school athlete, and then of the waterskiing accident which rendered him a quadriplegic and confined him to the wheelchair. Skip also tells of his faith in God and the support of his family, and what has happened since the tragedy. Then he challenges the audience to make the most of their God-given abilities—pointing out that too often we take health, talent, and even life for granted. Instead we should make the most of every opportunity and asset that we possess.

CLASSROOM SPEAKING DEFINED

In defining what classroom speaking is, let's clarify a couple of things that it is *not*. It is not using the teacher's desk as a *pulpit*. I will guarantee that if you go into the classroom with the idea that you're going to proselytize, your classroom speaking will be a disaster. You may have one successful experience, but it will be your last in that school, and you will close that school down for others in the near future. Even if a student asks a very specific question, resist the temptation to go into a full Gospel presentation. You are limited by law, and you are limited by principle. You are there to communicate some academics and to stimulate interest, so don't overstep your limits.

Nor is classroom speaking presenting Jesus as *an alternative*. Jesus is not an alternative, unless you want to say that heaven is an alternative to hell. Jesus is the solution. And whether or not you ever get to mention the name of Jesus Christ in the classroom (and many won't), don't go in with the idea, "I'm here to give you an alternative." You are giving them a different perspective, but it's not an alternative. It's the truth!

What, then, is classroom speaking? In a school setting, it is presenting biblical truths in a culturally relevant manner with academic credibility.

Bill Reif in *Discipling the Young Person*, Paul Fleischmann, editor (San Bernardino, Calif.: Here's Life Publishers, Inc., 1985).

As he concludes, the auditorium erupts with standing, enthusiastic applause. They have heard Skip Wilkins, and they will never forget him.

Many schools are open to having all-school assemblies which entertain and/or promote self-worth, friendship, school spirit, caring for others, courage to say no, and other positive traits. Middle schools and junior high schools are especially receptive to quality assembly programs. And there are many experienced, responsible, and Christian speakers and musicians who travel the country making these presentations.

These men and women will cost, but they are well worth the price, and usually the school will pay for the program. If not, local service clubs or businesses will often underwrite the expenses.

Because of the "separation of church and state," the speaker's in-school message will *not* contain any sectarian or controversial religious subject matter. This is very important because the school administrator goes out on a limb when hiring an outside speaker. It is also important because you want to return to the school with future programs or just to meet kids. If you gain the reputation as a valuable resource for the school, they will be open to future assemblies.

By performing in the school, the speaker or musician entertains and gives valuable advice to thousands of students. And because he or she is *good*, students will want to hear the speaker again. In the evening, therefore, you can have a special program or concert, *off campus and not sponsored by the school* where the person can perform and then share the Gospel.

Caution: Before hiring anyone, be sure to do your homework. Check references, especially administrators in the public schools where the speaker has recently performed.

There are many outstanding Christian speakers, entertainers, musicians, and others who are available for assemblies. Their programs include challenging talks, side-splitting humor, contemporary music, inspirational examples, and fast paced multimedia shows. For the names and addresses of these men, women, and organizations, contact your local Youth for Christ or Young Life office (or their national offices if there is no local chapter).

Materials
There are dozens of books and manuals on the market containing hundreds of crowd-breakers, games, activities, discussion starters, discussions, talks, songs, ideas, skits, and Bible

studies which can be used in a variety of settings.

Check with your denomination or with a Christian bookstore for their recommendations and an up-to-date list. I recommend the resources published by Scripture Press and Youth for Christ. The materials from Scripture Press may be purchased at Christian bookstores. The Youth for Christ resource manuals may be ordered by calling YFC sales, (312) 668-6600.

PROCESS
Whether the event is large or small, there are four steps you should take to be successful: *plan, arrange, direct,* and *follow through.*

Step #1—Plan
When planning any event, first you must *decide on your purpose.* This answers the "why" question. Ask: "Why should I (we) have this event?" and "What do I (we) hope to accomplish?" In other words, choose your goal. And it would be helpful to write a purpose statement and your objective.

As a purpose statement you could write, "The purpose of this meeting is to communicate the Gospel effectively to non-Christian high school students." Articulating your purpose will help you make important decisions about how to struc-

---

PUBLICITY REMINDERS

1. Check to make sure all the details are included and are accurate.
2. Let somebody else read it before it goes to press.
3. Don't be too proud to use the dictionary.
4. Get it out on time.
5. Keep mailing lists up to date.
6. Don't mix audiences; remember who's listening.
7. Don't skimp on the designing.

ture the program, where to have it, and who to invite.

Then your objective could be, "As a result of this meeting, students will accept Christ as their Saviour." This objective will drive the rest of the program because it begs the questions "Why will they respond?" and "How will they respond?" It will force you to structure the meeting to accomplish this objective.

Without clear purposes and objectives, meetings take on lives of their own, growing large and long and containing all sorts of irrelevant material.

A few years ago, Gail and I were asked to become involved in a banquet, the purpose of which was pre-evangelism or evangelism. As we entered the room, we were impressed with the setting and the decorations. And the program looked well-planned and focused, with an outdoor theme and a talk by a popular football coach. The food was excellent. Then the attention turned to the platform. After a skit and some outstanding music, the coach took the mike. He talked about football and then made a natural segue to his personal testimony, telling us about the difference Christ had made in his life. Afterward, the master of ceremonies explained how we could respond to the message we had heard. "This is great," I thought. "What a terrific way to share the Gospel!" And I prayed silently for my non-Christian friends in the audience.

Suddenly, however, the emcee directed our attention to envelopes in the middle of the tables, and he proceeded to give us a pitch for financial support. I was shocked and disappointed. Obviously the banquet planning committee had not thought through their purpose and objective, nor had they considered their audience.

Next, you should *design a preliminary plan*. This means thinking through the "when" and "where" of the event. Take out a calendar and circle the open dates, leaving enough time for making all the necessary arrangements. Consider the appropriate facilities—then check on their availability and price.

Then you should *think through your program*, answering "What will we do?" and "Who will be speaking or performing?" This will mean calling for the availability and costs of possible speakers, musicians, etc. and tentatively booking them.

Of course, in all of the planning process, you must remember the hoped-for audience. What are the needs of these young people; what will appeal to them? At a recent junior high event I attended, most of the program involved sitting and listening—the opposite of what energetic, enthusiastic, and short-attention-span early adolescents should have to endure. Instead, the activity should have featured high-energy games, a fast-paced schedule, and a short talk using a story or an object lesson.

You should also *design a preliminary budget,* looking especially for any hidden costs (see the "activity budget sheet" at the end of the chapter).

After deciding on your purpose, designing a preliminary plan, thinking through the program, and designing a preliminary budget, you come to decision time. You, and the rest of the planning team, should analyze the information you have collected (possible dates, locations, and program personalities and their costs) and see if they meet your expectations. If everything looks good, you will probably decide to confirm, send deposits, and mobilize the troops. If they don't, you will have to decide on a "plan B" or decide not to proceed.

Suppose, for example, that you heard that speaker Ken Davis was going to be in the area in a month and that he had an open date. You would have to decide whether or not that gave you enough time to line up an assembly and an evening program and to raise the money. Or suppose you had an ideal place and time available, but not the music group you wanted. You may choose to look for another group.

If you decide to proceed with your plans, you are ready to *determine the timing.* This means designing the program so that all the pieces are purposeful, relating directly to your objective. The best way to do this is to think through the meeting *backward.* Begin by deciding when the meeting should end. Then make sure you have enough time for the most important part, the communication of the message. If, for example, you have a guest speaker, and he needs twenty minutes, arrange the rest of the meeting around that non-negotiable block of time. As you work backward, then, from the most important ingredient, make sure the other parts of the meeting enhance the communication and do not detract from it. With the speaker mentioned above, it would be good to ask, "What can we do to set the stage for his message that will help him communicate?" Often I have been introduced to speak imme- diately after a skit that bombed miserably or a wild game; I had to work twice as hard to gain the attention of the crowd and to prepare them for the message. Whatever your content- communication vehicle—media, drama, speaker, discussion, music, film, etc.—make sure that the rest of the meeting flows toward it.

Another important part of the meeting which affects timing is *response.* Think through the end of the meeting and how you want the kids to respond—what you want them to do. If you want them to come to a counseling room, you will have to have the room, the time, and the counselors. If you want them to sign up for personal appointments, you will need cards, pencils or pens, and a system for distributing and col- lecting them.

The planning step concludes with *listing the other people you will need.* Because you now have a good idea of all that is involved in the program, you are ready to compile this list. Think through the meeting: before, during, and after. Your personnel needs will vary greatly depending on the program, but consider publicity, sales, arrangements, emcees, crowd control, media, counselors, cleanup, etc.

Step #2—Arrange
This step includes confirming the place and people for the program. Call, write, and send deposits if necessary. And make sure you receive a written confirmation of your arrangements.

"Arrange" means recruiting and assigning volunteers for the various tasks on your list. Begin by writing out what you expect for each assignment—then line up the helpers. This way everyone involved will know what is expected. When you ask someone to help with refreshments, give that person an index card which states how many cookies you need and when and where you want them. If you want someone to organize and run games in a gym, write that out and then

---

CROWD CRONTROL

How do you control a crowd of young people with an unlimited supply of energy? The secret is a combination of forecasting potential problems, careful planning, clear ground rules, fast action, determination to keep calm, and willingness to let them get away with a certain amount of rowdiness within *your* limits. Think through the meeting and activity to pinpoint potential problems:

1. *The meeting place*
   Is it the right size for your crowd?
2. *Troublemakers*
   Will certain individuals who have a history of causing trouble be there?
3. *Attention span*
   Is it short? Is the program designed to hold their attention (variety and fast-paced)? Spot possible lulls.
4. *The crowd-breakers*
   Which games lend themselves to rowdiness?
5. *The discussion*
   If you have one, are staff peppered throughout the crowd?
6. *The wrap-up*
   Is it interesting?

---

determine a time to get together to discuss possible games to use.

This step also means checking up—making sure that your volunteers are following through with their assignments. Don't treat these folks as children, smothering them with condescending attention. On the other hand, don't assume that they are doing everything right and on schedule. Call and say, "I just thought I'd check and see how you're doing with your job. Have you had any trouble with it?" It is also important to check on the interest level among young people. What kind of attendance can you expect? How can you get the word out to others? Do you have to make any adjustments in the program?

A time line will help you visualize when certain tasks should be done and when you should check with whom. Draw a line on a piece of paper. At the left end, write that day's date, and at the right end, the date of the event. Mark off the weeks between the two dates, and then write in red the important check points and the information you need at

---

CROWD-BREAKERS—HOW?

1. *Surprise the kids—not yourself!* Think the activity or skit through out loud. Say your lines ahead of time, so you know exactly how it's going to work. Go all the way through it step by step.
2. *Choose the right participants.* Choose lively, responsive people who will put on a good show.
3. *Program carefully.* Generally, it is advisable to do the "biggie" first; the opening crowd-breaker gets everyone involved, while later ones may be of the spectator type. This helps taper the excitement level.
4. *Give some thought to staging.* How much space will you need?
5. *Work on your timing.*
6. *Sell it!* You've got to be enthused about the crowd-breaker, or it will never work.
7. *Beware of the bomb.* If a crowd-breaker isn't working, be flexible and call it off.
8. *Be wise . . . be harmless.* In striving to have a fun time with kids, it is easy to violate our own standards of good taste. To do so is to be untrue to ourselves and to the Lord.
9. *Think up new ones!*
10. *Don't be afraid to repeat the winners.*

---

certain times. If you are selling tickets to a concert, for example, you will need to have a date where you determine whether or not you have sold enough tickets to continue with your plans. Other time-line events include printing handouts and posters, sending press releases, making phone calls, ordering materials, buying or making props, etc.

Step #3—Direct

This step involves the actual event. As the person in charge, you should make sure that everything and everyone is in place and ready to go. Ideally, you should be behind the scenes, with no other responsibility except to make sure that it goes well, like the director of a play or the conductor of an orchestra. This is especially important for large events or concerts involving a number of people and program resources. If, however, you are the emcee (like the Campus Life meeting described earlier), make sure that someone else is charged with the responsibility of coordinating the event. *Do not try to cover all the details from the front of the room while you are leading the meeting.* This includes bringing props to the front, keeping kids quiet, picking up used paper and pens, and preparing the refreshments. Others should be assigned those responsibilities.

Step #4—Follow Through

After the meeting, it is important to evaluate the event from

---

CROWD-BREAKERS—WHY?

1. Kids need something to relax them, to break down their barriers and prepare them for discussion.
2. Kids are social animals.
3. The leader builds rapport through his leadership of crowd-breakers.
4. Crowd-breakers are great image builders.

beginning to end. Hold a group discussion with your leaders and planning team or prepare a questionnaire. The purpose of the discussion or questionnaire is to determine whether you met your objectives and whether it was worth the investment of time, energy, and money.

Be careful, however, that the evaluation session does not degenerate into a time of critical nit-picking. One year we had a very successful Leadership Breakfast—over 600 high school leaders came on a Saturday morning to a hotel ballroom to eat, discuss leadership, listen to outstanding music, and hear a challenging speaker. The attendance was great, the food was good, the program was excellent, and the response was terrific! At the staff meeting the following Monday, after discussing what we liked about the breakfast, I asked what was wrong with it. Everyone found something small to correct, and soon it sounded as though this was the worst activity we had ever sponsored.

A better procedure is to ask: "What was good about the event? What did we do right?" Then you can ask: "What improvements should we make? How could we be more effective in reaching our objectives?"

The evaluation process should also include a discussion on whether or not to do another of these activities or one similar to it. You may want the event to be a one-time experience, or you may choose to continue to meet on a regular basis.

PUBLICITY TOOLS

1. P.A. announcements at school.
2. School newspapers.
3. Radio spots.
4. Event posters.
5. Image posters, stick-ons, jackets, shirts, bumper stickers, buttons, etc.
6. Mailers.
7. Handouts.

A friend in New Orleans wanted to have a ministry with young people, and so he met with a few high school friends before school on Fridays at McDonald's. Soon the word spread, and others came, so he enlisted the help of additional volunteers. Over the weeks the numbers grew until more than a hundred kids were gathering for breakfast, light entertainment, and a word from the Bible. Eventually, many accepted Christ as Saviour.

Besides evaluation, follow-through also means contacting *personally* and *individually* the volunteers who helped and the young people who responded. The volunteers need to be thanked for their efforts, and the young people need to be led along the next steps on the Christian path. Your plans should include how you will stay in touch with young people who respond to an invitation or who request personal conferences. Just make sure it happens. This will be discussed further in chapter 11.

If you are consistently building solid friendships with young people, you will meet their friends and associates. And you may develop a network of other Christian adults and young people who share your burden to reach young men and women for Christ. As you pray and plan together, you may see an opportunity for sponsoring larger programs and events. Planned and executed well, they can be effective tools for responsible evangelism.

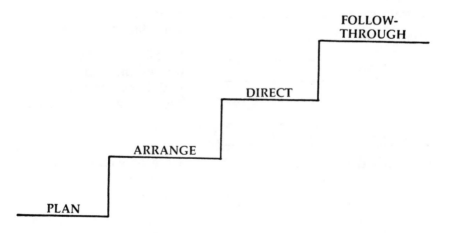

ACTIVITY BUDGET SHEET

NAME OF ACTIVITY _____

PERSON IN CHARGE_____

PURPOSE_____

OBJECTIVE_____

	EXPENSE		INCOME	
ITEM	Total cost	Per-person cost		
Rent (bldg.)	$____	$____	Ticket sales	$____
Speaker	____	____	Underwriting (donations)	____
Musician(s)	____	____		
Transportation	____	____	Misc. sales	____
Equipment	____	____	Registrations	____
Props	____	____	Other	____
Prizes	____	____		____
Printing	____	____		____
Advertising	____	____		
Postage	____	____	**TOTAL**	$____
Setup	____	____		
Follow-up	____	____	Expected attendance	____
Misc. (list)	____	____		
	____	____	Break-even point (attendance on which per-person cost is figured)	____
	____	____		
	____	____		
	____	____		
TOTALS	$____	$____		

Date filled out_____   Date of event_____

CHAPTER ELEVEN

Beyond Milk

The time has come. For most of a year she has waited, patiently enduring the awkward outward push of her abdomen and the uncomfortable and even painful inward pressure. But they were also months of joy, knowing that life had begun and was growing inside her; she felt him move . . . and kick. She knew that soon she would be able to hold, feed, and care for her little one. And those were months of planning—decorating baby's room, mapping the way to the hospital, choosing possible names, and dreaming. But now the waiting and preparation are over. Her body has said that it's time, and soon-to-be father and mother walk gingerly to the car and drive their practiced route.

It has been a long process . . . those nine months of waiting. But soon these parents will see and meet their new family member, their baby, their child.

With contractions at close intervals, the nurse pulls the bed and wheels it to the delivery room. The overhead light gazes down with its sterile glare, cold and shining steel bars hold her sides, and the soft swishing of baggy hospital garb and pungent antiseptic smells fill her senses. She is excited and afraid. Reassuring and confident words whisper through the hospital masks and warm eyes peer over them, allaying fears and helping her do what she must.

"Push!" says the doctor; then "Push again!" Soon the crown of a tiny head appears. Skilled hands pull the newborn into the light, shock her into reality, sever the former lifeline, and hand her with fresh tears to her mother's waiting arms.

Birth is a spectacular miracle, the grand finale of conception and trimesters of patience. And each new life is a reason for celebration. Mother and father marvel at their little one and together dream of what she will be and become.

But consider this possibility. Suppose the baby is born, placed in a crib, and then abandoned by parents, doctors, and nurses. Congratulating themselves on a job well-done, they leave the delivery room and move on to other concerns and responsibilities—perhaps even other conceptions, pregnancies, and births. We know the answer—left alone, without love, warmth, food, and protection, the baby would die.

Most certainly birth is the end of a long process and a great cause for celebration, but it is also the beginning of another life. And responsible, loving parents cradle their child and carefully feed and nuture her until she can eat and walk and live on her own.

No less a miracle is *re*birth—the entrance of a new soul into the family of God. The angels rejoice, and earthly parents "celebrate" eternal life. But these children also need tender care, helping them through their first steps of life. The science of obstetrics is important, but so is pediatrics.

The focus of this book is *evangelism*—introducing young men and women to the Saviour and leading them into a personal relationship with Him. Everything we have discussed thus far has centered around that goal—making contact, building friendships, talking seriously, explaining the Gospel, and using communication tools. And we pray that the Holy Spirit will work through us to bring many into God's family

But "responsible evangelism" also involves "follow-through care" (see chapter 4). We must be prepared to help these new babies in Christ find food and take their first steps in the faith.

THE PRECEDENTS

Jesus and the apostles had time for follow-through even though the millions in their world were waiting to hear just as much as in ours. Jesus told Peter and Andrew the first time He ever saw them, "Come, follow Me and I will make you fishers of men!" (Matthew 4:19) From the very beginning He made it clear that they were in for an extended experience of learning directly from Him. When He eventually left, Jesus told the Eleven, "Go and make disciples of all nations, baptizing . . . and teaching them to obey everything I have commanded you" (Matthew 28:19-20). It is not enough to bring about a confession of faith; that is only half of the Great Commission. The other half is follow-through.

Perhaps this is why the early church took it so seriously. When they were avalanched with 3,000 new believers in Acts 2, early church members didn't decide that they were too

---

WHO CARES?

Some time ago, half the population of a village in India, 558 people, embraced Islam. Asked why they preferred Islam to Christianity, the converts said that Christian concern for people ended with their conversion, while the Islamic society looked after them even following their conversions.

This illustration is a vivid reminder that there are differences between soul-winning (a term that punctuates many discussions about evangelism) and soul-caring. And these differences are crucial, not peripheral.

World Vision magazine, April 1982

busy for follow-through; "Every day they continued to meet together . . . " (Acts 2:46). Paul and Barnabas, at the risk of being restoned, "returned to Lystra, Iconium and Antioch, strengthening the disciples and encouraging them to remain true to the faith" (Acts 14:21-22).

Even that wasn't enough. After the Jerusalem Council, Paul said to Barnabas, "Let us go back and visit the brothers in all the towns where we preached the word of the Lord and see how they are doing" (Acts 15:36).

Years later, when Paul's name was known widely, he still refused to be a barnstormer, moving quickly in and out of town. He reminded the Ephesian elders of the three years he had spent with them and that he had "served the Lord with great humility and with tears, although I was severely tested by the plots of the Jews" (Acts 20:19).

Throughout his epistles Paul often spoke of his concern for the continued growth of people he had led to Christ, inviting them even to imitate him as an example of Christian living (1 Thessalonians 2:7-12; Philippians 4:9; 1 Corinthians 11:1; 2 Timothy 2:2).

Follow-through care was an integral part of the ministry of the early church.

"ISN'T THERE AN EASIER WAY?"

With all of the hours and money expended to get to know young people and bring them to the point of conversion, isn't that enough? Once they're in the kingdom, can't we breathe at least a little sigh of relief? Won't the Holy Spirit somehow work things out from that point on?

We know the answers to those questions. And even if we didn't know, we have proven by bitter experience that in follow-through care *we cannot just hope for the best.* Just as babies left to themselves on the delivery table are in serious trouble, our spiritual children are wide open to the infections of frustration, discouragement, misinterpretations of Scripture, and ridicule. We've heard stories about great men and women of the faith who survived on nothing more than a tract handed them after a rally or a Bible in a motel room. Maybe we should never have heard those stories. They represent the few spiritual survivors who scrambled to the surface, but they are the exceptions.

The rule is that a young person who walks down an auditorium aisle, raises a hand, or signs a card, but is not subsequently loved and nurtured by his spiritual parent and other family members, may get just enough religion to "innoculate" him for the rest of his life. And he may brush aside the Holy Spirit's conviction with, "Yeah, I tried that Jesus business once, but it didn't work." He will be virtually immune to the real thing. Others who have made a genuine commitment to Christ will stay immature in the faith unless they are helped and encouraged to grow.

We cannot expect machines or books to do our work. Well-meaning Christian individuals and organizations often assume that all they have to do is write a letter to a new believer or give him or her a book or booklet to read. There's nothing wrong with writing letters to kids who have just accepted Christ or giving or loaning them books. In fact, any thorough program of follow-through care will probably include both of these. Many excellent books have been written for beginners in the Christian life. But not everyone will read, especially not every teenager. Even if they do, a lot of the information won't soak in. There's no way they can ask a book their questions. One-way, impersonal communication is not enough.

We cannot get everything done by mass indoctrination. Some Christians hope to wrap things up (including all the necessary follow-through care) in one fell swoop at some kind of large meeting. This may help, but it won't do the whole job. Again, it is too impersonal. A relationship cannot blossom through only a single meeting and then occasional contacts.

We refused to indoctrinate the young person *before* her conversion, allowing her to make up her own mind. Why should we think differently *after* her commitment? She is still a unique human being who needs more than an injection from our theological hypodermic needle.

We should not delegate the job unless it is absolutely necessary. Follow-through is sometimes seen as another person's speciality or else as very elementary work to be shoved off on someone else. It is true that newborn babies can survive when handed to a foster mother . . . if she knows what she's doing and cares enough about the baby to actually do it. But too often new Christians have been lost or permanently damaged because the foster parent to whom he or she was assigned was incompetent or didn't really care.

The best arrangement is for the new Christian to be loved and trained by her actual spiritual parent. She needs you now more than before she became a Christian. Back then, she was responsible for her own problems; now you've brought her into a radically different way of life, and it's up to you to make sure she gets all that you told her she'd get when she accepted Christ.

This does not mean that she talks only to you. She needs to feel the warmth and support of many Christian brothers and sisters, including some her own age. You should encourage friendships with other believers and involvement in church and in various Bible studies; but the basic responsibility is yours. You brought about her birth. Now you must see that she grows.

If you cannot continue to be her parent, be sure to choose a foster parent as close to you as possible.

When does follow-through with a new Christian begin? It begins almost without us even realizing it—the minute the young person finishes inviting Christ into his or her life. A new life has just been born; he needs immediate attention.

The need is so great at the beginning that we do not have to wait for him to request appointments with us; we should go ahead and make them happen. We should take the lead.

FOLLOW-THROUGH TIMETABLE
Stage One: Immediate Follow-through
The purpose of stage one is to confirm the decision the young person has made.

Immediately following the prayer to accept Christ, we should talk to the newborn Christian about assurance. (This was mentioned briefly in chapter 8.)

We should show the new believer that his relationship with Christ is based on what the Bible *says*, not on what he *feels*. This involves giving him a copy of the Bible (a recent trans-

CONFIRMING YOUNG PEOPLE

The personal ministry of evangelizing culminates in confirming that "new baby" in God's family. The issue here is not formal confirmation, but a personal confirming him in the "what next?" of trusting Christ.

The *event* of rebirth is *the beginning of a lifelong process.* Now that this new relationship with God has begun, how do you develop it?

First, be sure he has a Bible and that he writes in the front the date of his "spiritual birthday." That "birth certificate" can be a real encouragement on the days when the doubts come. Then help him set some goals for the first seven days of knowing Christ.

A. *Start a notebook*

That is a spiritual diary in which he will record what the Lord says to him through the Bible each day for the next week.

B. *Write a letter*

To whom? To Jesus! This will help him begin the process of communicating with this Person he has just come to know.

C. *Go to church*

Be with God's people this Sunday. Take notes on the sermon, looking for a personal application.

D. *Tell someone*

"It is with your mouth that you confess and are saved" (Romans 10:10).

E. *Find a buddy*

Team up the new Christian with a more mature Christian from his own age-group. It will help them both!

Ron Hutchcraft in *Evangelizing Youth,* Glenn C. Smith, ed. (Wheaton, Ill.: Tyndale House Publishers, Inc. 1985).

lation) to keep and use and explaining that this is God's reliable message to all of us.

Begin by showing him the table of contents, and suggest that he start reading each day beginning with 1 John and then James (check the books off on the contents page and mention the page numbers so he's sure to know how to find them). Don't suggest a certain number of verses or chapters to read; leave him on his own at first because he may go tearing through large sections just to see what it's all about.

The other question in the back of his mind is probably, "Has anyone else ever done what I've done? Am I really weird for having prayed with this guy? Who else is really a Christian?" So tell him stories of other young people who have found Christ. Encourage him to tell someone about his decision (another Christian young person or adult friend). It would also be helpful to give him a booklet or pamphlet which explains what just happened to him. Christian bookstores will have many of these from which to choose.

And encourage him to pray, talking to God in his own words . . . about anything.

Then set up an appointment to meet with him in a day or two during which you will check to see how things are going and if he has any questions.

Conclude by praying for him. Also, unless his parents are Christians, advise him not to make a big announcement at home ("Guess what—I just became a Christian!"). Most parents will misinterpret those statements of faith-discovery ("What do you think we are . . . heathens?"). Instead, encourage him to let the folks *see* the change in his life rather than hear about it.

Stage One: Within 72 hours

This is the first appointment you'll have after the young person has made a decision to follow Christ. Talk about the literature you gave him. Did he read it? Did he disagree with any of the points?

Then talk about his Bible reading. Did he get into 1 John at all? What did he think of it? What questions does he have? Did he really understand that this is God talking to him? If he has finished reading the two epistles, move him next into the Book of Mark, the shortest and most brisk of the biographies of Christ.

Try to determine generally how the person's life has been going. Is he perplexed about any emotional ups or downs? Have his parents said anything? Should they have a chance to meet you? How has prayer worked so far?

In reality, you are verifying his decision to follow Christ, especially if he responded in a group setting or was counseled by someone else. Before you begin any elaborate system of follow-through, you should make sure that the person really did experience conversion.

When I took a group of young people to see a Christian film in a large theater downtown, Larry stood and walked down the aisle in response to the invitation given after the film to those wishing to give their lives to Christ and to talk with a counselor. Later he told me that during those few minutes backstage, he tried to listen over the rising sound of the other whispered conversations and actually prayed some kind of prayer. Then he shook hands with the counselor, took the piece of literature, and joined us in the lobby. A few days later, when talking to Larry, in what I assumed would be a "follow-through" situation, I discovered that he had not yet made his decision. After extensive conversation, I was able to lead him to Christ.

Because of the lack of time, the setting, and the poor communication, many "seekers" go through the motions and have not actually made a genuine commitment. And they may end up even more confused than before receiving "counseling." Don't assume that the young person has accepted Christ; talk to him or her about it yourself.

During this appointment, it is also important to explain how to have a daily "quiet time" of Bible study and prayer. And give him a follow-through booklet. *Lessons on Assurance* published by the Navigators (reprinted as *Guaranteed in Writing* by Youth For Christ) is an excellent one. Others are available at Christian bookstores. Explain how this book will help answer important questions asked by kids like himself. Tell him that it spells out the most basic things a new Christian should know

However structured, we must relate closely with one another. There are ways this can be encouraged in the regular worship services, even in formal, sacramental settings. Auxiliary meetings offer other opportunities for fellowship, especially in small-group gatherings. In this connection, the Sunday School provides many options. Emphasis must be given to the home and family in the program. Through it all, personal relationships need continual cultivation in the ongoing discipling process.

This is crucial in helping new believers get established. In their first steps of faith, they are particularly vulnerable to doubts and temptations and need someone with them to give counsel. How fortunate when this person can be a more mature Christian with whom they already have some identity. That the church has often neglected such guardian care explains why so many converts fall away or at least never seem to grow in the likeness of their Lord.

The Master Plan of Discipleship by Robert E. Coleman (Tappan, N.J.: Fleming H. Revell Co., 1987).

and that you would like to study it with him. Then set up a weekly time to get together, either just the two of you, or in a small group for new Christians. If, for example, a number of kids respond to a large activity that you have sponsored, you could form a small group to go through the material together.

Explain the importance of church; and if he doesn't have a church and his parents wouldn't mind, offer to go with him to one or to take him to yours.

Checklist for Stage One
Within 72 hours of his or her commitment to Christ, the new Christian should:
- be assured that he or she is a Christian,
- own a recent translation of the Bible or New Testament,

● begin thinking about a church to attend,
● have a follow-through book to work through (like *Guaranteed in Writing*),
● have an appointment set with you (or a small group) to study the follow-through book.

Keep the following hints and cautions in mind:

1. Reviewing the plan of salvation from the witness tool is helpful.

2. Remember that the young person goes home. Be very sensitive to his or her parents.

3. Make sure you set up the next appointment.

Stage Two: Basic Follow-through Program
Your purpose in stage two is to help the young person gain confidence in his or her new relationship with Christ.

This stage focuses on the completion of the first, basic follow-through material that you gave him. It should be completed within two weeks and can involve three appointments or three small group meetings.

Guaranteed in Writing, for example, has five lessons. Lesson 1 can be done together, and then you can assign Lesson 2 as homework. When you get together again, you can check Lesson 2, fill out Lesson 3 together, and assign Lesson 4 as homework. During the third appointment, you can review Lesson 4 and work on Lesson 5 together.

During these Stage Two appointments, you should review the new Christian's commitment to Christ, making sure that he understands what happened and answering any questions. And you should encourage him to attend church with someone. It would also be very helpful for him to plan to explain how he became a Christian to a friend. This means putting into his own words what he did and what happened to him.

One of the most rewarding ministry experiences I can remember was teaching a group of high school guys. All four of these high school juniors had become Christians at our summer camp. We met together weekly to work through the follow-through material. They grew by leaps and bounds as they studied the Bible together and then held each other accountable during the week.

"PRAYER IS BORING"

Incredibly, that's the conclusion that many Christian young people have come to. And they've come to that conclusion for three reasons.

● First, we've mostly taught prayer as something deeply personal and private.

● Second, what corporate, public praying most Christian young people have experienced *has* been boring.

● Third, we've talked about prayer *at* young Christians. Often we've failed to do it *with* them. Perhaps, because we know so little ourselves.

Prayer Pace-setting, by John Earwicker (London: Ebenezer Baylis and Son, Ltd., 1987).

Checklist for Stage Two
Within two weeks of his or her commitment to Christ, the young person should:
● complete a basic follow-through booklet like "Guaranteed in Writing,"
● memorize five verses in the booklet,
● have assurance of new life in Christ,
● attend church with a friend,
● begin praying daily,
● begin reading the Bible daily.
   Bear in mind the following hints:
   1. Show him or her how to use the Bible.
   2. Show him or her how to find the verses and memorize five of them.
   3. Check up with him or her often. If a young person drops out, review the plan of salvation and discuss problems.
   4. Tie the new Christian to another Christian young person

(sort of a "buddy system") for fellowship and accountability.

Stage Three: Ongoing Bible Teaching Program
Your purpose at this stage is to help the young person begin to grow spiritually. This means plugging the young person into a regular program of Christian fellowship and teaching. Obviously a strong local church would be ideal. There he can hear the Bible taught from the pulpit and in Sunday School.

While waiting in the airport last month, a woman came up, looked closely, and said, "Dave Veerman? Are you Dave Veerman?"

I recognized her, but I couldn't remember her name. After she told me who she was and that she had been in my Campus Life club more than fifteen years ago, it all came back. Jan had been a troubled young girl who had come to Christ through my ministry. There were several follow-through appointments and counseling talks, but then she went to college and I moved out of town. We had lost touch with each other.

Turning to her daughter at her side, Jan said, "Lisa, this is the man who introduced me to Jesus." Then she told me more about her life and how she was active in church.

As I left Jan to board the plane, I was thrilled that she had continued to grow in her faith without me. And then I realized why; it was the church. By becoming involved with a caring body of believers, she had surrounded herself with love, help, and spiritual nourishment.

For whatever reason, we won't always be there to care for these young people. But the church will. Every community has those who believe in Christ and local churches where God's Word is faithfully proclaimed. We must help new believers understand the necessity of linking up with the rest of the body of Christ.

If, however, the individual's parents would object to his attending a church other than theirs, you will have to use another plan. Here are some possibilities.
● Plug into a nearby Campus Life, Young Life, or Fellowship of Christian Athletes group, especially the sessions designed for Christian growth (for example, Campus Life has "Insight" meetings and Young Life has "Campaigners" groups). These

---

GROUP CLASSIFICATION

Although there are thousands of groups in existence, each of them could be classified into one of three different categories based on their purposes. Groups are formed to accomplish a joint task, foster mutual relationships, or influence members to change their behavior and attitudes.

The purpose of a task group is to accomplish a job that could not be done effectively by a person working alone. The focus is on the task itself.

The relationship group focuses on the human need for companionship. The emphasis here is on the members and their interaction with one another.

An influence group is composed of people who meet together for the shared purpose of changing their behaviors and attitudes. The sucess of this group is evidenced by its impact on the lives of the members.

In actuality, every group is a combination of the three types noted. The variable becomes their *emphasis* in the group. The individuals who compose a group may have different purposes for joining, and the leader will need to focus on each of the aspects at different times in the life of the group in order to accomplish its ultimate goal.

Getting Together: A Guide for Good Groups, by Em Griffin (Downers Grove, Ill.: InterVarsity Press, 1982).

---

organizations will be especially helpful if they include a majority of kids from the new believer's school.
● Find a good church youth group that will be nonthreatening to the parents and get him involved with the kids there.
● Begin your own small group in which you can cover basic Christian growth topics. These topics should include: the lordship of Christ, the concept that Christ is interested in the whole person, Bible application, how to deal with conflict,

sharing our faith, the purpose and importance of church, and others.

During this stage and the months and years to follow, you will continue to be this person's friend, and your relationship will develop and deepen. Because of this, you will have many opportunities to answer questions, offer counsel, and trouble-shoot for and with him. It is important to remember, howev-er, that your ultimate goal is for him to *stand alone in his faith.* In other words, just as it would be unhealthy for an adult child to be tied to his parents' apron strings, still totally de-pendent on them for food and other necessities, so too with our children in the faith. They need to grow, mature, and "leave the nest."

One way to help this process is to get the person involved in a student leadership training program where kids are trained to share their faith with their friends. This will be covered in the next chapter.

Checklist for Stage Three
Within 6 to 12 weeks, after completing the follow-through program, the young person should:
• continue having a regular quiet time,
• attend church regularly,
• complete the basic lessons on Christian growth,
• be developing a good reputation as a Christian,
• be invited to a student leadership training program.
   Keep in mind the following hints and cautions:
   1. At this stage, checking up is essential. If a young person misses a session, arrange an appointment to cover the lesson with him or her individually and renew the commitment.
   2. Anyone who has faithfully reached this point should be invited to join a student leadership training program.

THE RESULTS
The ministry of follow-through care is in no way drudgery; it's the scene of some of the most exciting spiritual changes. We know that we are making an impact on young lives when we see kids evidencing:
• new attitudes toward people (their parents, brothers, sis-

ters, friends, teachers, employers); they're not so mad at the world,

● new attitudes toward the Scriptures; the once-dead Book begins to speak to them,

● open talk about their new life; they bring up the subject in conversations with us and others,

● reevaluation of values and moral guidelines; they start asking, "I wonder what God thinks about my doing this?"

We should also point out these observations to the young person, who, strangely enough, may be oblivious to the profound changes in his or her own life. The "good kid" especially may think that nothing has really happened in her life until we start asking about some of the above.

When we begin to see these results, we know that the initial experience was genuine and that growth has begun.

Follow-through care is a ministry which is nonnegotiable. As important as our ministry of evangelism is, we must also be concerned with discipleship—helping these new converts grow in their faith, moving them toward lifelong service to Christ. We dare not leave our babies on the delivery table.

CHAPTER TWELVE

Pass It On

Sitting in the hotel ballroom, I shifted to a more comfortable position to hear the announced youth choir. "It only takes a spark," they sang.

I listened politely, thinking that they certainly looked sincere even if their sound wasn't the best I had ever heard. And secretly I wished they would finish so we could get to the speaker. Our Youth for Christ staff conventions were notorious for marathon meetings, and this was turning into one.

After the song and the requisite applause, a petite young lady in the choir's first row (a soprano I guessed) walked to the microphone and stated simply and clearly, "I'm a junior in high school. Last year I began to come to the Campus Life meetings for my school, and four months ago I accepted Christ as my Saviour. Thank you for caring for kids like me."

As she turned to walk back to her place in the choir, another girl stepped to the mike. "That was Sandi," she said.

"Sandi told me about Jesus, and now I'm a Christian too. Thank you."

On her heels came Holly and then Kristen, each one bearing testimony of a communication chain which had begun with Sandi.

Other "chains" were also identified as each member of that teenage choir explained how he or she had decided to follow Christ during the last six months. And each one thanked us for our organization and our commitment to the ministry.

They finished with another song, and as they left the stage, the standing ovation bore strong proof that their message was heard and appreciated. I don't remember who spoke that evening, but after 20 years, I still remember the choir and the chain-reaction effect of the Gospel.

Paul may have been Super Evangelist of all time. But he knew he had to teach other people to do it. He recorded his "multiplication table" in 2 Timothy 2:2, "And the things you have heard me say in the presence of many witnesses entrust to reliable men who will also be qualified to teach others."

That's the spiritual relay team that carries the torch much farther than any single runner could do alone. No strategy for reaching local young people can ignore the dynamite potential of the Christian kids themselves. They are not *supplemental* to an evangelism strategy . . . they are *fundamental!* There is no more powerful witness in the youth culture than a spiritually alive young person. And yet most reborn Christian kids are fans, not players out on the field. Why isn't the explosion of the Gospel being detonated by the kids themselves?

Ron Hutchcraft in *Evangelizing Youth*, Glenn C. Smith, editor (Wheaton, Ill.: Tyndale House Publishers, Inc., 1985).

MULTIPLICATION

A wise father once asked his young son to make a choice of how he would like his allowance. He could have a dollar a week, or he could begin with a penny and then double it every week. Thinking quickly, the boy soon figured that in four weeks, he would have four dollars by the first method, but only eight cents by the second. He enthusiastically answered, "I'll take the dollar!"

"That's too bad," said his father. "Now, after sixteen weeks you will have received $16. If you had taken the penny, after sixteen weeks you would have received $337.67. And soon you would have taken everything I own!"

That's multiplication, and it is an important principle of evangelism. We can have a terrific ministry, reaching kids one by one; but if we teach them to be evangelists, to win their friends to Christ, think of the multiplying effect our ministry will have! And considering the need, we can't afford to do anything less.

COMMUNICATION

Teaching young people how to tell their friends about Christ also makes sense because of the natural communication channels they have. As we have discussed in previous chapters, we adults must overcome age and cultural barriers to communicate effectively with teenagers. But these "natives" already know the language . . . and they have the communication networks.

Tim played guard on the varsity football team. An excellent athlete with a warm personality, Tim was popular with his teammates. They elected him co-captain for the next season, his senior year. Tim was also a Christian. That summer, Tim went to our Campus Life camp, and he got Jeff, the other co-captain, to come with him. Through the steady witness of Tim and the talks by the camp speaker, Jeff committed his life to Christ.

After returning home, Jeff told his girlfriend about his new faith, and she also accepted Christ. Eventually almost half of the football team became Christians through Tim, Jeff, and others. The contacts and relationships were already in place,

I became a Christian through the influence of a girl named Ruth. She wasn't the designated leader of our young people's group. As a matter of fact, I was! But in terms of real influence, Ruth had the clout. It's been said that there are four classes of group members:

1. Those who make things happen.
2. Those who watch things happen.
3. Those who have things happen to them.
4. Those who don't even know things are happening.

Ruth was in the first category. She was attractive, vivacious, with a contagious enthusiasm for God. For most of us, high school is a time of cliques, trying to be part of the in-crowd and avoiding the jerks. But Ruth moved from group to group with ease. To her, everybody was a good friend.

I was in the fourth category—at least spiritually. Although I was elected president of the youth group, I had no knowledge of the Lord. The only time I'd ever opened our family Bible was to press my biology leaf collection. It was the biggest book on the shelf. If someone had asked me if I was a Christian I would have looked at him or her quizzically and said, "Sure. I try to be a nice guy." But it wasn't an issue. No one asked.

Em Griffin in *Getting Together: A Guide for Good Groups* (Downers Grove, Ill.: InterVarsity Press, 1982).

and Tim and Jeff used them as bridges for sharing the Gospel.

LOCATION

Jack Hamilton would often ask us "professional" youth workers, "Where is the Holy Spirit on the high school and junior high campus?" We would answer that, of course, He is in the lives of all the Christians there. Then Jack would challenge us to train those Christian students to share Christ with their friends. After all, they're already positioned to do so.

It's true! Potential Christian missionaries are already in place in the mission field. Sitting in classrooms and cafeterias, rubbing shoulders in the halls, and cheering at the games, these students have daily contact with hundreds of young people who need Christ. But they need to be mobilized—motivated, challenged, taught, sent, and counseled.

Who are these potential missionaries? In reality, any Christian young person qualifies. They may be members of your church, they could be new believers, the results of your personal evangelism efforts, or they may be your children. Whoever you choose to train, make sure that you see it as a team effort. Don't announce to young people that *they* must witness and you will help them. Instead, approach them with the understanding that *you and they* should be sharing the Gospel with peers. Then talk to them about working together to do just that.

SENSITIZE STUDENTS

The first step in mobilizing young people for effective communication of the Gospel is to help them realize that their friends are lost in their sins, unfulfilled, hopeless, and hell-bound without Christ.

My daughter Kara is in seventh grade. She has grown up in a Christian family (with a father who has been deeply involved in an evangelistic ministry for her entire lifetime). She has attended Sunday School, worship services, and other special events at the evangelical, Bible-believing churches we have attended. And yet, until recently, she had no real understanding that her friends were not Christians in the true sense of the word. This is *not* an indictment of our family or our churches. The fact is that junior highers are just out of grade school and haven't learned to make sophisticated and conceptual divisions among people. And high schoolers are not that much different. Unless they have been fed a steady diet of altar calls, they don't really understand that their friends really *need* Christ.

One of the exciting results of Kara's involvement in our Campus Life/JV program has been her growing sensitivity to the spiritual needs of her friends.

Vision has to have ownership. Students may run on your vision initially, but you need to help them develop their own vision. That will come about progressively as they spend time doing the work of the ministry, internalizing Scripture and developing convictions within their own hearts.

Chris Renzelman in *Discipling the Young Person*, Paul Fleischmann, editor (San Bernardino, Calif.: Here's Life Publishers, Inc., 1985).

New believers, of course, are another story! Fresh from their own decision to follow Christ and overflowing with enthusiasm, they want to tell the world! Already motivated, they will have to be channeled.

Other young people, however, you will have to challenge. You can do this most effectively by studying the Bible together, seeing what Jesus said about "seeking and saving," etc., and allowing the Holy Spirit to work in their lives. It will also be helpful to ask questions about specific kids—their personal struggles and their direction in life. Love for Christ and for their friends will motivate most Christian young people to share the Good News.

ENCOURAGE THEM TO PRAY

The first step in winning anyone to Christ is to pray for him or her. Too often we mistakenly begin by training young people in witnessing methods or techniques. Then they begin to rely on their own cleverness. We must remember that salvation is a work of God through the Holy Spirit, and we are only His instruments.

In the church youth group one Sunday evening, we high schoolers were challenged to bring the Gospel to our friends. Thoroughly motivated, I pledged to tell five kids a day about the Lord. And I really gave it my best shot. But soon I was tired, disappointed, and defeated. In reality, I was talking to the wrong kids (any unsuspecting "victim," not those whom the Holy Spirit was preparing), for the wrong reasons (to feel good about myself and to please my youth director), at the wrong time (I was not being led by the Spirit either), under the wrong power (my own determination, not God's strength), and with the wrong message (that they were going to hell; instead of sharing what Christ was doing in my life). No wonder I became totally disillusioned with witnessing.

Gospel communication must be bathed in prayer; therefore, we should encourage our kids to pray . . . for themselves (confessing any sin and keeping the relationship with God fresh and vital), for their friends, and for opportunities to tell their friends about Christ.

Ask them to write down the names of all their friends. Then have them choose five to ten of them and write their names on a "prayer list." Challenge them to pray each day for these individuals, that God will be working in their lives, preparing them for the message, and that God will provide communication opportunities.

One summer I hosted a special seminar series in my home. For six consecutive Tuesday evenings, eight high school students faithfully came to be taught how to "give away their faith." The first night, we made prayer lists and committed ourselves to consistent prayer for these friends. Over the weeks, and then the months that followed, it was exciting to hear reports of answered prayer as one by one the people on our lists gave their lives to Christ: Beth with her teammate; Craig with his college roommate; Denise with her sister; and others.

At the same time, I was involved in Friday morning prayer breakfasts sponsored by Christian Businessmen's Committee (CBMC). Unlike many "prayer" breakfasts where we never seem to get around to praying, these gatherings centered around men praying for their non-Christian friends and associates. First we would submit names of those for whom we wanted the group to pray. Then we would gather in threes or fours, get on our knees, and pray for those on the list. From week to week it was thrilling to hear that men and women for whom we had been praying had become Christians.

TEACHING BY EXAMPLE

"Part of the evangelism training for youth includes class-room instruction. But it's not enough to hold classes on witnessing. Youth must be *shown* how to witness. They should learn by observing an experienced person evangelizing someone else."

John Musselman, "Training Youth for Evangelism," *Working With Youth*, (Wheaton, Ill.: Victor Books, 1982).

Another effective method is "prayer triads"—three young people praying consistently with and for each other, and holding each other accountable. Be a catalyst for forming triads.

TRAINING YOUNG PEOPLE

After a young person has been sensitized to the need and has begun to pray for others, he or she is ready to be trained. This training should include knowing the right attitudes, approaches, and answers.

Attitudes

As mentioned in chapter 8, evangelism is *"one beggar telling another beggar where to find bread."* In other words, when we tell others about Christ, we should be sharing how He met our need and how He can meet theirs. Evangelism is *not* getting on our soap box and telling others that they are *wrong* . . . or approaching people with the condescending attitude that we are better than they are . . . or even presenting a list of facts from the Bible.

The truth is that *all* have sinned (Romans 3:23)—that includes us and all other Christians as well as those whom we seek to reach. When we are motivated by love for Christ and love for others, it will show in our attitudes. We will exude concern, care, and compassion and others will be drawn to us and to the Saviour.

As Ron Hutchcraft says, "Witnessing is introducing our friend on earth to our Friend in heaven."

We should also be aware that young people will have mental barriers and fears to overcome. They may fear rejection by a person or a certain crowd; they may fear being labeled a "fanatic"; or they may be afraid that they won't know what to say.

The only way to overcome these fears is to face them (admitting that they exist and are normal), to pray about them, and to work on them together. Help the young person realize that witnessing should be a natural part of everyday conversation, not a memorized speech. And also help him or her understand that God is responsible for the results, not us. We aren't salesmen, paid for getting customers to sign on the dotted line. Instead, we are ambassadors, representing the King of kings. And if people decide not to follow Christ right now, we shouldn't pressure them or take it personally. We should continue to love and pray for them.

Approaches

Acts 1:8 records Christ's promise to the disciples that they would be His witnesses *after* the Holy Spirit came upon them. Effective evangelism, therefore, is a by-product of God working in our lives. Jesus also said that "No one can come to Me unless the Father who sent Me draws him" (John 6:44). In other words, God is also working in the lives of those who will respond to the Gospel message.

We should communicate to our young people, therefore, that effective witnessing is God *bringing together two people for His glory*. This means that we should be looking for the opportunities He gives and depending on His strength, not relying on our cleverness or worrying about how to slip the Gospel into a conversation.

Witnessing begins with a lifestyle that reflects Christ. If we are tuned-in to Him and living as He desires, people will be drawn to us and to "what we have." When talking to a new Christian after school one day, she said, "Recently everybody seems to be coming to me with their problems. They want me to help them." I explained that although it probably wasn't obvious to her, since she had accepted Christ, she was a more loving and caring individual. Her friends could see the difference; they knew she cared about them and would try to help. That's one of the differences Christ makes in our lives.

And if we are asking God to give us opportunities to tell our friends about Christ, He will. It may be the person telling about his family problems, the friend confessing that she doesn't know what to think after discussing literary pictures of hell in English class, a classmate who is really depressed and confides that he wonders about the purpose to life, or someone who is curious about what the speaker said at the church youth group. Our responsibility is to be sensitive to His leading and then prepared to tell what we know when the occasion arises.

Answers

It is also important to give young people *content* to share. First Peter 3:15 states: "Always be prepared to give an answer to everyone who asks you to give the reason for the hope that you have. But do this with gentleness and respect." God will give us opportunities, but we must be prepared to take advantage of them.

A MINISTRY LIFESTYLE

The Great Commission is not a special calling or a gift of the Spirit; it is a command—an obligation incumbent upon the whole community of faith. There are no exceptions. Bank presidents and automobile mechanics, physicians and schoolteachers, theologians and homemakers—everyone who believes on Christ has a part in His work (John 14:12).

From *The Master Plan of Discipleship* by Robert E. Coleman (Tappan, N.J.: Fleming H. Revell Co., 1987).

Over the years I have learned another principle of evangelism: *God will lead me to those whom I can help with what I know.* There are two sides to this truth. On the one hand, it means that God can use me today, now, as I am. I don't have to go to another seminar or learn more facts in order to be used by Him. There are people who need to hear *my* story.

Young people, especially brand-new Christians, need to understand this. Often they feel inadequate and think that they have to be thoroughly trained before they can share their faith. Instead, they can begin to tell others right away.

It's amazing how God uses our knowledge and experiences. One Friday evening I was reading a column in a Christian magazine. The writer commented how certain scholars had disputed the canonicity of Esther and Song of Solomon because they contained no direct references to God. He then refuted that idea by showing how both books were filled with the presence of God. I put the magazine away and didn't think about it the rest of the evening.

The next day, I drove to a camp to speak at a youth retreat. After one of my talks, I asked if there were any questions. Totally "out of the blue," one of the counselors asked: "What do you think about Esther and Song of Solomon and the fact that they do not talk about God?" Because that column was fresh in my mind, I was prepared to answer that question.

That was not just a coincidence. (And, by the way, no one had ever asked me that question before that weekend or has ever since then.) God led me to someone I could help with what I knew.

If there is any group that can spread good news to others, it is youth. When young people begin to realize the power and love of Christ in their lives, they do not hesitate to spread it to everyone they meet.

From *The Basic Encyclopedia for Youth Ministry*, by Dennis Benson and Bill Wolfe. (Loveland, Colo.: Group Books, 1981).

But there is a flip side to this principle: The more I study and learn about God and His Word, the more people He can lead me to.

We should encourage our young people, therefore, to share their faith *now* and not to wait until some future date when they will be fully prepared. But we should also encourage them to study and learn all they can (2 Timothy 2:15).

Here are some suggestions for training young people in the content . . . the "what" and "how" of sharing their faith.

• Study the previous chapters of this book with them, especially chapters 5, 6, and 8. Teach them how to initiate and build relationships and how to "cross the bridge." Share your strategy and teach them how to use the "Your Most Important Relationship" booklet or other tract.

• Have them write out a testimony. This should be a simple explanation of how the person accepted Christ. An easy outline to remember is "B.C." (what his or her life was before Christ), "the decision" (what drew the person to Christ and how he or she responded), and "A.D." (what his or her life has been like after the decision).

• Role play witnessing situations with the individual. Take turns playing the roles of "non-Christian" and "Christian." The "non-Christian" should ask what a Christian is and how to become one. Then the "Christian" should attempt to share the Gospel and lead him or her to Christ.

• Fill out the "World of Influence" sheet together (printed on page 195). Be sure to fill one out for yourself also.

• Use other resource materials. See your pastor and Christian bookstore for recommendations. Youth for Christ's "Campus Life Guide to Student Leadership" is excellent. This is a booklet with nine lessons which can be used individually or in a small group. And Youth for Christ/Canada (phone: 416-243-3420) has produced a six-part, interactive video series entitled "Touching My World." Its purpose is to help youth share Christ with their friends.

BE A COACH

The last step in teaching young Christians to share Christ with their friends is *coaching*. This involves an ongoing relationship

WORLD OF INFLUENCE

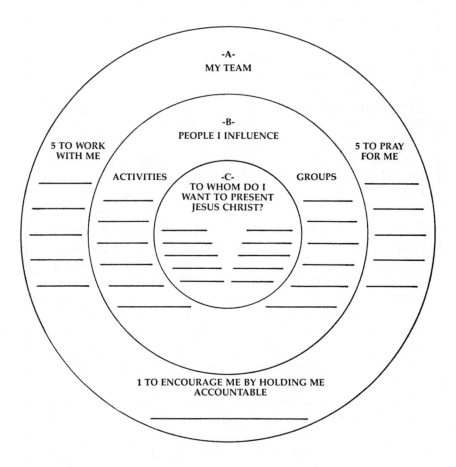

A CASE IN POINT

Sherri Howard is a young woman, now 19 years old, who has taken a dream and commitment very seriously. In July of 1985, at Youth Congress '85, Sherri believed that God wanted her to make an impact for Jesus Christ in her school, her city, her state, and her country. She has done just that.

Sherri is now the director of an organization called Choice Lifestyle, in Wichita, Kansas. The sole purpose of Choice Lifestyle is to challenge and mobilize young Christian students to do three things: (1) read their Bibles daily; (2) carry a Bible to school; and (3) organize prayer and Bible study groups in schools.

There are now well over 4,000 students who are committed to these responsibilities whom Sherri has recruited through high school assemblies and concert programs. The exciting dynamic presentation is led by Sherri and three other sharp teenagers doing drama, music, and serious talk about choices that young people must make.

I recently had the privilege of experiencing in person a dynamic presentation by Sherri and her troop. It was a spiritual uplift. These kids are living on the cutting edge of faith that is active and courageous. Her dream was more than a fleeting thought. It has substance that challenges me—a 40-year-old "professional youth worker." Go for it, Sherri—and don't let us slow you down!

Youth for Christ/USA—Rolly Richert, Vice President of Communications

---

between you and the young person—praying, encouraging, trouble-shooting. He or she needs to know that you will be there when needed and that you are holding him or her accountable. Ideally, you will be working as a team (along with other Christian brothers and sisters) to reach youth for Christ.

A friend of mine has "discipled" many young people. After leading them to Christ, she has nourished them carefully from God's Word. And then she has taught them how to share Christ with others. This woman is not a flashy, upfront, charismatic leader. But in her quiet way, she has seen hundreds come to Christ through multiplication. Her secret, she says, is staying in touch with these kids—prodding, encouraging, praying, and helping.

In teaching kids to pass it on, to share the faith with their friends, we ignite a torch which can light the whole world.

CHAPTER THIRTEEN

Questions You May Be Asking

The following questions and answers deal with common situations which you may face in your own efforts to share the Good News with the young people in your world.

Q: What should I do if a parent violently opposes this "Christian thing"?

A: Hopefully this won't happen because you will have met the parents and communicated your intentions to them. I have found that most parents are upset when they *don't know*. Then they imagine the worst and answer their own questions about who I am and what I am doing. But if they know me, usually they will assume the best and call me when they have questions. Presently, for example, I am working with junior highers in a Campus Life/JV club in my neighborhood. Often parents will thank me for what I am doing for their kids although I'm sure they don't know everything about Youth For Christ or our meetings. They trust me because I am a neighbor, the parent of their children's friend, and a friend myself.

If there is a parent, however, who strongly opposes you and who threatens legal action or something similar, you should stop seeing the young person. Continue to pray for him or her and leave the rest to God.

A situation may arise where you learn of an abusive home or you think a young person may be suicidal, and you don't feel you can, in good conscience, drop out of the person's life. In this case, when you are opposed by the parent, get legal advice. You should know the risks and the courses of action you can take.

Q: How do I deal with kids from Jewish families?

A: This is an area which requires much sensitivity and care. Although most Jewish young people are not very involved with their religion, their parents don't want them to consider any other. Usually these parents are very concerned about who is influencing their children and about anything that even sounds "Christian." If you don't know the family and your primary contact with the young person is one-on-one, it would be good to meet the parents as soon as possible to introduce yourself and to explain your involvement with their child. If during the discussion the question of religion comes up, don't try to hide the fact that you are a Christian, but use nonthreatening explanations of what you doing and terms like "discussion," "Bible study," "understanding who God is and how He fits into our lives," etc. Another way to reach the Jewish young person is through a small group, but even here it is important to be very open and aboveboard with parents. Of course the most effective way would be through another young person.

Q: How should the approach to senior highers and junior highers differ?

A: There are some significant differences between these two age groups which should affect how we minister to them.

Senior high kids are much more independent than junior highers. Parents know that soon these children will be away from home, and so senior highers begin to move away emotionally. Parents also tend to give more freedom, with less restrictions on their time and activity. Junior-high or middle-school young people, however, are still seen by their parents as children, and so Mom and Dad are usually still quite involved in their lives. Another factor influencing independence is the car. Most high school students have their licenses, but Mom or Dad still have to chauffeur the younger kids.

This independence factor will affect the ease with which you can get together with young people, the activities in which you participate together, and the involvement of their parents.

This is obviously a generalization, but the main focus of most high school students is "identity." They are struggling with who they are and where they fit in. They need therefore, to be encouraged, affirmed, and accepted. In contrast, most early adolescents, need is to master certain life-skills. They want to know *how to* make friends, *how to* play basketball, *how to* talk to adults, and so forth. This will affect what you discuss in groups and what you choose as your point of contact with them.

Most junior highers do not think conceptually. This means that discussions about grace, love, and "purpose in life" will bore them. Instead, they would love to talk about boys or girls, how to use a computer, and fashion. On the other hand, juniors and seniors in high school will find conceptual discussions quite interesting.

Older kids can relate to others fairly well on an individual basis although it will take time to gain their friendship and trust. Junior highers look up to adults and still have respect for them and their authority. They will listen to you, *but* they will have trouble relating one-on-one. Building relationships with these younger kids will be more effective in small groups (e.g., four guys going to a game together, three girls going to the mall, etc.).

It is generally true that the older a person gets, the longer he or she is able to sit and listen. No programs should be boring but, as a rule, any programs for junior highers should change every five minutes or so. Unless it is a gripping story or film, they won't sit still. Their young minds and bodies are growing, and hormones are churning. Early adolscents need action and variety. Do something with them—don't just sit and talk.

Q: How can I get these young friends into church?

A: It will not be difficult to get the new Christian into church if he or she does not come from a strong church background, has a friend who is a Christian, or would match culturally and socially the people at church. If a young person has the characteristics listed above, you will simply have to suggest that he or she accompany you and/or the friend to church on Sunday. With no religious background, the parents probably will not object, and with no social or cultural barriers, the young person probably will not feel out of place.

If, on the other hand, the person does not match that general description, you will have to adjust your strategy. For those who have been active in a church in the past or whose mom and/or dad still have a loyalty to a certain denomination or religions, you will have to communicate carefully with the parents. Assure them that you are not proselytizing their children or undermining their authority. And invite them to come also.

If there are social barriers (e.g., the young person is from another country or looks quite different than your average church member), you will have to take time to prepare the church for his or her arrival and educate the young person about all the cultural trappings he or she will encounter.

Q: What if they ask questions I can't answer?

A: Just admit that you don't know but you will try to find out and get back with them. You might even suggest that the two of you look for the answers together (in the Bible, in a book, with a pastor, etc.).

Q: How can I start a youth ministry in my community?

A: The first step is to find other Christian adults who also have a deep desire to see young people come to Christ. This group could center around a neighborhood, a school, or a whole town. While doing this, you should contact the pastors of evangelical churches near you. Tell them what you want to do and ask for their guidance, help, and names of those who might be interested. Next, set up a meeting where you can discuss your dreams, expectations, and philosophy of ministry. It would be helpful to have information about various Christian youth ministries at that meeting (e.g., Youth for Christ, Young Life, Fellowship of Christian Athletes, Campus Crusade for Christ, and others). If you decide that one of these organizations would be the best match for you and your situation, you could contact them for further guidance.

Even if you don't design and organize officially, this group of adults can be an invaluable network of prayer, support, and personal ministry.

Q: How can my whole family be involved with me?

A: It is important that your ministry with young people not come at the expense of your family. Make sure that they understand what you are doing and why. It would be best to make this a family project. If you have older children, you can work with them to reach their friends. Or you and your spouse could work as a team. Your spouse and children can pray regularly for you and for specific individuals. And whn you have kids in your home from time to time, everyone in the family should know why and be invited to help.

Q: How can I stay in touch with youth culture, their music, styles, stars, etc.?

A: The best way to find out what kids are like is to be with them. Go to school events and hangouts; talk to them. Also you can talk with teachers, coaches, youth workers, and other youth-serving professionals. A record store will have lists of the "top 40" hits, and you can always listen to the more popular radio stations. A periodic glance at *MTV (Music TV)* or *VH-1 (Video Hits One)* on cable will provide insight as well. And there are always the teenage magazines (like *Seventeen* or *Teen*). You may want to subscribe to *Teen Vision* and *Youth Worker Update* (see the Resources section), monthly newsletters loaded with information.

EPILOGUE

It was my first trip to the city . . . or perhaps I should say *the* city—New York. My tourist itinerary included a myriad of sights, experiences, and wonders, but none was more important than the world's tallest building; I had to see it. My friends and I hailed a cab, jammed inside, and gave the driver our desired destination.

What a ride! It was chaos. Swerving around cars and through red lights and honking the horn incessantly, the cabbie rushed recklessly through the traffic. We pitched, rolled, held our breath, and questioned our chances for survival. Finally the harrowing adventure ended—curbside at the entrance to the Empire State Building.

Visibly shaken, we peeled out of the cab, muttered prayers of thanksgiving, and walked on unsteady legs into the massive edifice. After riding the elevator as high as it would take us, we climbed the stairs to the observation deck.

I stepped to the rail, carefully leaned over, and looked down. There before me lay the city and her streets. From my new vantage point, everything seemed so orderly and purposeful. Automobiles stood in neat lines at corners. When the lights changed, the cross traffic stopped and they moved forward. There was no noise, and even the cabs seemed under control.

Only minutes before, crammed between bodies in a New York City cab, my small world seemed chaotic and out of control. But perched well above the asphalt, cement, sweat, and ear-splitting yells and honks, life seemed calm and orderly. My perspective made the difference.

This book is about perspective, a way of seeing. At first I introduced the world of adolescents, helping you see their needs, understand their crises, and feel their pain.

Next I challenged you to become a part of the solution, breaking through the religious clutter and cacophony, reaching lost young people for Christ. These kids need you!

Then we saw evangelism from a biblical perspective, understanding that all we do must be consistent with God's Word. Biblical evangelism means *responsible evangelism*—person-centered and Spirit-led.

Drawing closer to the ministry itself, we looked at its nuts and bolts . . . the how-to's: establishing friendships, building relationships, counseling individuals, explaining the Gospel, using small groups, planning larger programs, helping young believers grow in their faith, and teaching kids to share Christ with their friends.

Now it is time to look at the whole picture, to put all of the puzzle pieces together. This means seeing the evangelism of youth from God's perspective.

The fact is God loves those kids more than we ever could, and He longs for them to enter His family. And God wants to use us to reach them.

That's the key verb—*use*. We can contact and build and meet and preach. We may even be honored publicly for our dedication to youth. But unless the ministry is His, our work will be empty. That's the point. It must never be our work, it must be His. Praying every moment, we should step out in faith, always sensitive to His leading. Psalm 127:1 reminds us: "Unless the Lord builds the house, its builders labor in vain."

So take a long look at your world, from God's perspective. Open your eyes to lost and hurting teenagers; look at your abilities, talents, and resources. See God's purpose for placing you in that neighborhood and in those relationships, and watch the Holy Spirit use you to spread the Good News about Christ.

RESOURCES

FOR MEETINGS

Campus Life Magazine Leader's Guide—Published by Christianity Today, Inc., the Leader's Guide comes each month wrapped around the regular issue of *Campus Life*. Each one has six meetings which are tied to articles and themes in the magazine, Extras (lists of ideas), and other resources. For subscription information, write to *Campus Life*, 465 Gundersen Drive, Carol Stream, IL 60188.

Any Old Time Series from Victor Books (a division of Scripture Press)—A 12-book series featuring ready-to-use meetings for junior and senior high youth. Each meeting includes crowd-breakers, discussion questions, a Bible study, a wrap-up, and optional activities.

Serious Fun and *More Serious Fun* by Dave Veerman (Victor Books)—Organized by topic in a resource format, each book contains hundreds of crowd-breakers, discussion starters, discussions, and Bible studies. For Scripture Press materials, visit your local Christian bookstore or call (312) 668-6000.

Youth for Christ/USA Ministry Resource Manuals (Vol. 1–5)—Each one contains hundreds of crowd-breakers, evangelistic meetings, and Bible studies. Volumes 1–3 are in separate meetings; volumes 4–5 are in a resource format. Youth for Christ also has two volumes of curriculums for junior high ministry (geared for non-Christian young people). Called *Campus Life*/JV, each volume contains 5 sets of 5 weekly meetings and a big event. Write to YFC Sales, Box 419, Wheaton, IL 60189, or call (312) 668-6600 for more information.

Other publishers of materials for youth ministry include David C. Cook (850 N. Grove Ave., Elgin, IL 60120), Moody Press—Sonlife Ministries (820 N. LaSalle Drive, Chicago, IL 60610), Group (P.O. Box 481, Loveland, CO 80539), SonPower Youth Sources (1825 College Avenue, Wheaton, IL 60187), and Youth Specialities (1224 Greenfield Dr., El Cajon, CA 92021).

ASSEMBLY PROGRAMS

Camfel Productions—For many years this Christian organization has produced outstanding multimedia programs for use in schools and other youth gatherings. Each program is high quality and contemporary and focuses on a current need of young people. Their address is 136 W. Olive Ave., Monrovia, CA 91016.

Ken Davis—An outstanding comedian and speaker, Ken is the premier high school assembly speaker in America. He entertains and challenges kids to accept themselves and to reach their God-given potential. He has also spoken for churches, junior highs, retreats, camps, conferences, and conventions. Ken can be reached at 6080 West 82nd Drive, Arvada, CO 80003, (303) 425-1319.

Ed Kilbourne—Ed has a style of his own. Skillfully crafting accoustical guitar chords around his words, Ed writes and performs his own songs and many contemporary favorites. A fine musician, Ed is first an accomplished communicator as he talks of love, relationships, and the meaning of life. To book Ed Kilbourne, write him c/o Fly-by-night Records, 1811 Burkin Rd., McConnells, SC 29726.

Freddie Langston—A one-man, high-energy, high-tech concert, Freddie plays keyboards, electronic drums, and guitar, and he sings. His musical tastes range from current rock and pop favorites to contemporary Christian selections. Freddie is also an excellent speaker. He can be contacted at Papa's Dream, Inc., Box 11575, St. Petersburg, FL 33713

Mars Hill Productions—A Christian film company, they have a number of short films on the felt needs of young people. These can be used in a variety of settings. *The Question*, an award-winning film about teen suicide, works well in assemblies with someone who can answer questions afterward. For their catalog, write to Mars Hill Productions, 9302 Wilcrest, Houston, TX 77099, or call (713) 879-9800.

Harold Morris—Featured on the radio program *Focus on the Family*, this Christian ex-con has a powerful and captivating story to tell. He has spoken for thousands of high school students and has written *Twice Pardoned* (Word Books). If you can't book him, consider using the video presentation of his assembly speech (also excellent for evangelistic meetings). Contact *Focus on the Family*, Pomona, CA 91799—(714) 620-8500.

Motivational Media—Jim Hullihan, the founder of Camfel, is the creative genius behind this organization which produces multimedia programs and discussion-starter films. Their address is 148 S. Victory, Burbank, CA 91502.

Becky Tirabassi—With an energetic, effervescent, sparkling personality, Becky tells of her experiences with popularity and drinking. She has spoken for young people, adults, and youth leaders nationwide and is the author of *Just One Victory* and *Quiet Times* (Tyndale House). She can be contacted at *My Partner Ministries*, Box 8862, Orange, CA 92664.

Skip Wilkins—A quadriplegic who has overcome tremendous suffering and adversity, Skip is an inspiring speaker and well-received by students everywhere. He tells his story in his talks and in a book, *The Real Race* (Tyndale House). For more information, write to Skip at 2104 Cocoa Circle, Virginia Beach, VA 23454.

DISCIPLESHIP TOOLS

Christian Life Series by Jim Burns—This series offers student workbooks entitled *Putting God First, Making Your Life Count, Living Your Life as God Intended,* and *Giving Yourself to God.* A Christian Life Series leader's guide is available also. Published by Harvest House Publishers, 1075 Arrowsmith, Eugene, OR 97402.

Moving Toward Maturity Series—This series features five student books which take high-school age students through the basics of Christianity. Barry St. Clair has authored the books which are titled *Following Jesus, Spending Time Alone with God, Making Jesus Lord, Giving Away Your Faith,* and *Growing On.* Each book has an accompanying leader's guide to facilitate group discussions. Book 4 in the series has an accompanying tract, *The Facts of Life,* and follow-up booklet, *Getting Started.* Published by Victor Books, 1825 College Ave., Wheaton, IL 60187.

NEWSLETTERS

Search Institute—122 West Franklin, Suite 525, Minneapolis, MN 55404, (612) 870-9511.

Teen Vision—P.O. Box 4505, Pittsburgh, PA 15205.

Youth Worker Update—1224 Greenfield Drive, El Cajon, CA 92021.

RECOMMENDED READING

Aldrich, Joseph. *Life-Style Evangelism*, Portland,Ore.: Multnomah Press, 1981.
   This outstanding volume teaches how to witness to our
   peers by living for Christ.

Barton, Bruce, Ron Beers, Jim Galvin, LaVonne Neff, Linda
   Taylor, and Dave Veerman, eds. *Practical Christianity*,
   Wheaton, Ill.: Tyndale House, 1987.
   This reference work on Christian growth contains hun-
   dreds of articles from scores of writers including Jill and
   Stuart Briscoe, J.I. Packer, Josh McDowell, Richard Fos-
   ter, Janette Oke, R.C. Sproul, and others.

Benson, Dennis and Bill Wolfe, eds. *The Basic Encyclopedia for
   Youth Ministry*, Loveland, Colo.: Group Books, 1981.
   This is literally the "A to Z" of youth ministry, with
   hundreds of helpful suggestions and tips.

Cheney, Lois. *God Is No Fool*, Nashville: Abingdon, 1969.
   This little volume is filled with profound and challenging
   devotional thoughts for adult Christians.

Coleman, Robert E. *The Master Plan of Evangelism*, Old Tappan, N.J.: Fleming H. Revell, 1963.
   Dr. Coleman analyzes Jesus's approach to evangelism in
   the New Testament, and he draws applications for contemporary evangelistic strategies.

Coleman, Robert E. *The Master Plan of Discipleship*, Old Tappan, N.J.: Fleming H. Revell, 1987.

This is an analysis of the discipleship practices and patterns of the early church as recorded in Acts.

Collins, Gary R. *Christian Counseling: A Comprehensive Guide*, Waco: Word Books, 1980.
As the title indicates, this book contains helpful counsel on counseling for just about every occasion—a valuable resource.

Colson, Charles. *Who Speaks for God?*, Nashville: Thomas Nelson, 1985.
This is a collection of some of Chuck Colson's most provocative and insightful editorials.

Dausey, Gary, ed. *The Youth Leader's Source Book*, Grand Rapids, Mich.: Zondervan, 1983.
This book covers the waterfront of youth ministry, beginning with how to lay the foundation for a successful youth ministry and including sections on developing a ministry environment, providing purposeful activities, and others.

Deyo, Art, ed. *The Whole Person Survival Kit*, Wheaton, Ill.: Youth for Christ, 1976.
This is an operations manual for youth ministry volunteers.

Earwicker, John. *Prayer Pace-Setting*, London: Ebenezer Baylis and Son, Ltd., 1987.
This British veteran Youth for Christ worker sets forth a practical plan for mobilizing young people for prayer.

Engel, James. *What's Gone Wrong With the Harvest?* Grand Rapids, Mich.: Zondervan, 1975.
In this scholarly, yet practical, analysis of evangelism, Dr. Engel carefully outlines the persuasion and decision-making process.

Fleischmann, Paul, ed. *Discipling the Young Person*, San Bernar-

dino, Calif.: Here's Life Publishers, 1985.
An excellent resource for youth leaders, the chapters are written by a number of outstanding ministers including E.V. Hill, Bill Stewart, Wes Hurd, Becky Pippert, David Busby, Bill Reif, and others.

Griffin, Em. *Getting Together: A Guide for Good Groups*, Downers Grove, Ill.: InterVarsity Press, 1982.
Dr. Griffin is a professor and a veteran youth worker who has led and taught hundreds of small groups. From his knowledge and experience, he shares insights and instructions for organizing and running effective small groups.

Griffin, Em. *The Art of Christian Persuasion*, Wheaton, Ill.: Tyndale House, 1981.
Here Dr. Griffin gives an overview of the research into "persuasion," and he makes application to the church for evangelism. It is a valuable source on how to communicate effectively.

Jones, E. Stanley. *A Song of Ascents*, Nashville: Abingdon, 1968.
This book chronicles the spiritual journey of this great missionary to India and man of faith, and it contains tremendous insights into cross-cultural communication.

Kesler, Jay and Ron Beers, eds. *Parents and Teenagers*, Wheaton, Ill.: Victor Books, 1984.
This 700-page reference work has hundreds of articles on just about every conceivable topic relating to parents and teens—a practical resource parents and youth workers. The authors include: Howard Hendricks, James Dobson, Tony Campolo, Kenneth Gangel, Charles Swindoll, Evelyn Christenson, and many others.

Kesler, Jay, Ron Beers, and LaVonne Neff, eds. *Parents and Children*, Wheaton, Ill.: Victor Books, 1986.
Written as a sequel to Parents and Teenagers, this book is

geared to parents of younger children through the junior high years. Some of the authors include: Gene Getz, Tim Hansel, Kevin Leman, David and Cheryl Asby, Charlie and Martha Shedd, Paul Lewis, and many others.

Little, Paul. *Know Why You Believe*, Wheaton,Ill.: Victor Books, 1984.
Although it was written in the '60's, this book still gives the most helpful answers to the basic questions posed by searching nonbelievers.

Little, Paul. *How to Give Away Your Faith*, Downers Grove, Ill.: InterVarsity Press, 1966.
This practical volume covers the basics of witnessing.

Olson, Keith. *Counseling Teenagers*, Loveland, Colo.: Group Books, 1984.
This is an excellent resource for anyone working with adolescents. Focused on teenagers, it offers invaluable insight and practical advice to those who counsel.

Pippert, Becky. *Out of the Saltshaker*, Downers Grove, Ill.: InterVarsity Press, 1979.
Strongly motivational and peppered with lively illustrations, this book presents a biblical and practical approach to sharing the Gospel.

Spotts, Dwight and David Veerman. *Reaching Out to Troubled Youth*, Wheaton, Ill.: Victor Books, 1987.
Written for those who want to reach delinquent or predelinquent young people, this book explains how to understand them, how to communicate with them, how to discipline them, how to handle problem situations, and much more.

Strommen, Merton P. and A. Irene. *Five Cries of Parents*, San Francisco: Harper and Row, 1985.
The Strommens have gleaned much from their exhaustive study of early adolescents and their parents. This

study by The Search Institute was finished in 1984, and they have summarized and published their conclusions in this book. It contains profound insights into the thoughts and feelings of junior-high-age young people and their parents.